Advance praise for

Guide to Sea Kayaking
in Maine

"This guide has a wealth of information on where to paddle, how to paddle safely, and how to preserve access to the coast and the islands."

—Christopher Cunningham,
Sea Kayaker magazine

"If you're planning on sea kayaking in Maine, this book is every bit as important as your boat, paddle, and PFD."

—Eugene Buchanan,
Publisher, *Paddler* magazine

Help Us Keep This Guide Up to Date

Every effort has been made by the authors and editors to make this guide as accurate and useful as possible. However, many things can change after a guide is published—establishments close, phone numbers change, facilities come under new management, etc.

We would love to hear from you concerning your experiences with this guide and how you feel it could be improved and kept up to date. While we may not be able to respond to all comments and suggestions, we'll take them to heart and we'll also make certain to share them with the authors. Please send your comments and suggestions to the following address:

The Globe Pequot Press

Reader Response/Editorial Department

P.O. Box 480

Guilford, CT 06437

Or you may e-mail us at:

editorial@globe-pequot.com

Thanks for your input, and happy travels!

Regional Sea Kayaking Series

Guide to Sea Kayaking in Maine

*The Best Day Trips and Tours
from Casco Bay to Machias*

by

Shelley Johnson and Vaughan Smith

The
Globe
Pequot
Press

Guilford, Connecticut

Copyright © 2001 by The Globe Pequot Press

Cover design: Adam Schwartzman
Text design: Casey Shain
Cover photograph: Jim Dugan
Map design by: Mary Ballachino
All photos courtesy of Shelley Johnson and Vaughan Smith

Library of Congress Cataloging-in-Publication Data
Johnson, Shelley, 1954–
    Guide to sea kayaking in Maine / by Shelley Johnson and Vaughan Smith. — 1st ed.
       p.   cm.—(Regional sea kayaking series)
    Includes bibliographical references.
    ISBN 0-7627-0746-1
    1. Sea kayaking—Maine—Guidebooks.   2. Maine—Guidebooks.
I. Smith, Vaughan. II. Title. III. Series.
GV776.M2 J66 2001
917.4104'44—dc21   00-067771

Manufactured in the United States of America
First Edition/Second Printing

To all who serve as stewards
and protect Maine islands

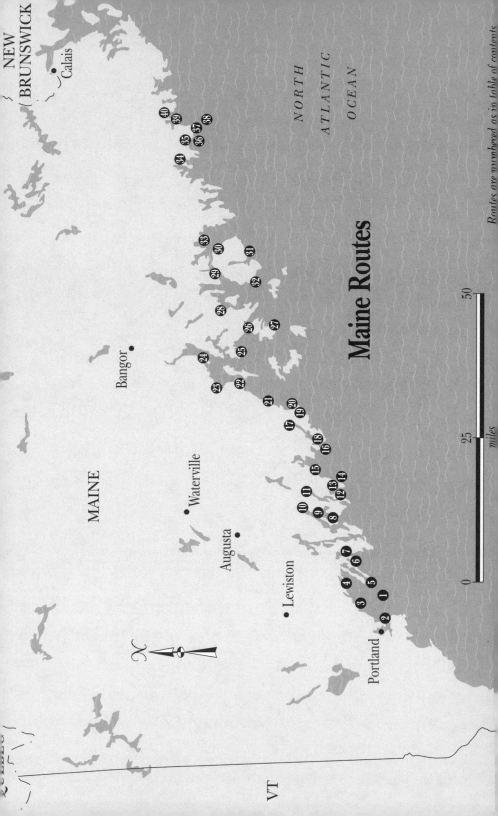

Maine Routes

NEW BRUNSWICK

Calais

NORTH
ATLANTIC
OCEAN

MAINE

Bangor

Waterville

Augusta

Lewiston

Portland

VT

Routes are numbered as in table of contents

miles

0   25   50

Contents

Tenants Harbor to Camden

Lincolnville Beach to Stockton Springs

Castine to Blue Hill

Mount Desert Island and Frenchman Bay

Downeast: Milbridge to Machias

Appendices

Acknowledgments

No task is ever completed without utilizing the knowledge and wisdom of others in the field. Maine is blessed with a caring and careful paddling community that has set many of the safety and low impact standards in practice throughout the country today. People like Ken Fink, Tom Bergh, Matthew Levin, Natalie Springuel, Marc Bourgoin, and Dave Mention have worked hard for many of these guidelines and set fine examples as professional guides and instructors.

The staff and members of the Maine Island Trail Association (MITA) give countless hours to protect and nurture the islands of Maine. If this resource weren't so thoughtfully cared for by these people, a guidebook like this would be meaningless. MITA's executive director, Karen Stimpson, and past executive director, Cate Cronin, have been invaluable sources of information over the years about Maine's islands, their peculiarities, and their unique issues. Steve Spencer of Maine's Bureau of Parks and Lands is not only an avid sea kayaker, but as the state's recreational specialist overseeing the public lands on Maine's coast and islands, he has played a major role in setting the standards by which this resource is successfully managed.

We would also like to thank Lee Bumsted for her helpful resource, *Hot Showers! Maine Coast Lodgings for Kayakers and Sailors,* which we would highly recommend for any small boater needing lodging options and travel tips as they explore the Maine coast.

We would like to thank Jeff Serena, our editor, whose support and good humor helped us through the stress points that any project has.

Finally, we'd like to offer a heartfelt thanks to Dave Getchell, Sr.: a visionary and tireless worker for water trails in his own Maine backyard and throughout North America. Dave has managed to convince private and public landowners that public access can actually foster stewardship and protect the resource. It just requires some thoughtful attention.

Map Legend

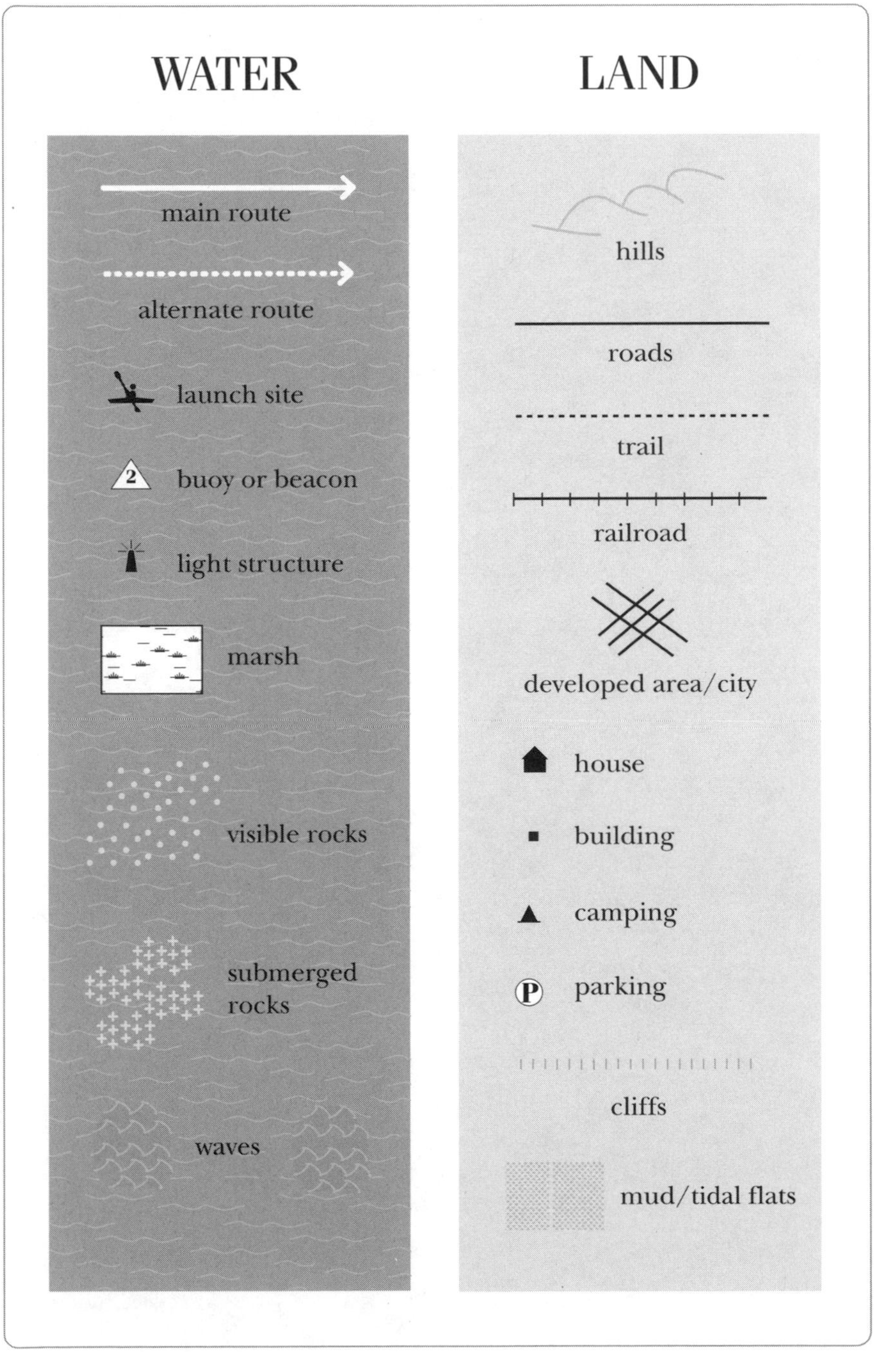

WATER

→ main route

⇢ alternate route

🛶 launch site

🔺2 buoy or beacon

light structure

marsh

visible rocks

submerged rocks

waves

LAND

hills

roads

trail

railroad

developed area/city

🏠 house

▪ building

▲ camping

Ⓟ parking

cliffs

mud/tidal flats

The Coast
of Maine

There are many reasons why the coast of Maine is considered one of the top sea kayaking destinations in North America. Maine offers a complex and convoluted coastline that, if straightened, would stretch some 3,000 miles. The shoreline from Cape Elizabeth to West Quoddy Head is extraordinarily beautiful, combining the rugged textures and subtle shades of granite with the pointed, deep green of spruce trees. There are so many nooks and crannies to explore that it would take several lifetimes to soak up all they have to offer. Simply glance away from the mainland shore and you will be enticed by islands, so many that experts still argue over an exact number.

Humans are by nature drawn to islands. Their very separateness is intriguing, and the satisfaction of reaching their shores under our own power is deeply rewarding. Each Maine island is unique and has its own story to tell of cataclysmic weather, human influences, and the ebb and flow of its own ecosystems. Islands feel wild even when they're not; their isolation from the mainland heightens our sense of escape and can calm even the most urban-frazzled souls.

Maine's islands also create complex boating conditions as winds and tides stir a sea studded with these impediments to the easy flow of air and water. The seas may rip and swirl as they find their way around an island or spend their energy on one shore, leaving the other side placidly unaware. Paddlers need to be wary of an environment this challenging. Yet these same complexities make Maine's coastal waters exciting to sea kayakers and sailors alike. After all, a millpond gets boring after a while. Anyone plying these waters, whether sea kayaker or container ship captain, must rely heavily on local knowledge.

Maine's waters are chilly and rich in the nutrients which support an array of aquatic culture and the birds and mammals that feed off them. Many islands and patches of shoreline represent the edges of a particular species' range. Quite often, an island will be closed to visitation during seabird nesting season, which coincides with much of the paddling season. A good set of waterproof binoculars is a must for exploring the coast of Maine.

Maine's rockbound coast is a geologist's delight. It speaks of glacial activity and a receding ice cap that left behind a series of narrow peninsulas and drowned river valleys in the midcoast region and broad bays and larger islands in the downeast region. This dynamic past has given the coastline its amazing range of shapes and textures. A bird's-eye view would allow you to see these formations and discover that islands from the midcoast to the downeast coast regions are the nearly submerged tops of ancient folded bedrock. Glacial activity can be seen in the deep scratches that were carved into the granite on some shorelines as moving ice sheets crushed rock and dug their edges into the bedrock underneath. These scratches run along the north–south axis of the glaciers' movement. You might even encounter a glacial erratic along a mainland or island shoreline. These are the boulders that were carried and then later discarded a long way from their original home by the melting ice sheets. Ballast stones—man-made versions of erratics—may also litter shorelines where trading ships disgorged their rocky ballast, often from some foreign shore, before taking on a load of Maine timber or quarried granite.

The beauty and natural history of coastal Maine are not the only features that tempt sea kayakers to explore these shores. Coastal villages and towns nestled in coves and protected from full exposure to the weather are a luxurious retreat with their restaurants and lodging establishments. Maine has offered services to travelers and sportsmen for hundreds of years; even our license plates tag us as VACATIONLAND.

As a sea kayaker you'll have a unique perspective on this magnificent landscape and the people who live and work in it. Skirting the shore of a manicured estate, watching a lobsterman bait and set his traps, or tagging along behind a windjammer as she sets sail from her home port—you're an intimate observer from the cockpit of your kayak. Enjoy it all!

Safety Guidelines

Paddling conditions in Maine range from placid to heart pounding, sometimes over the course of the same day. The complexity of this coastline and the ever changing weather present an array of challenges for sea kayakers as well as rewards. Unless you are hugging an accessible shoreline in benign conditions, your kayak should have bulkheads or flotation bags both fore and aft, or should be a sit-on-top design. The smaller recreational models with their open interiors are great for the lake and flatwater rivers but present a hazard when paddled offshore, where a reentry after capsize may be difficult at best.

Since Maine weather changes rapidly, you'll want to pack along a variety of clothing that is suitable for the water and air temperatures you'll encounter. A wet suit or dry suit is a must on the edges of the paddling season, because water temperatures don't begin to reach the midfifties until at least mid-June. As water temperatures increase in early July, you may choose to shift into quick-drying layers that are windproof and waterproof, depending on the nature of your trip. Make sure to pack a hat that can warm you and protect you from the sun.

It's rare to find potable water on any of the islands, so you'll want to pack along plenty of your own. We always keep a water bottle accessible during paddling and another one or two tucked into the hatch where they are cooled by the colder water passing beneath the hull. You'll certainly want to slather on the sunscreen at regular intervals. When there is a cooling sea breeze, you may not realize that your skin is still getting cooked! You'll appreciate a good pair of polarized sunglasses; just make sure that any glasses have retaining straps.

Navigation

Familiarity with a chart and compass will make any trip more relaxing and educational. Many of the trips in this book hug the shoreline, where staying found is relatively easy, but being able to refer to a chart and note your actual course not only is safer but also leaves you with a worthy souvenir. As you leave the easy identification of the mainland shore, you'll need to be able to use navigational aids as checkpoints and be able to plot a course using bearings to fixed objects or landmarks. As you look seaward toward an island group, it is often hard to distinguish a given land mass. Paddling a course that you plotted in advance will save you time and the aggravation of heading off the most efficient line of travel during a crossing. It is also invaluable to be able to use a range—an alignment of two fixed objects, one behind the other, along your course. In this way you can make early and easy corrections for the effects of wind and tidal current.

Assisted and Solo Reentry Skills

When you paddle offshore, you must be comfortable with the process of getting back into your boat in the event of a capsize. Without the safety net of a nearby shoreline or other boaters, you're on your own. While a capsize may be rare for most sea kayakers, the place to learn reentry techniques is not when you experience your first unexpected capsize. Take at least a full-day course of instruction that allows you to practice these techniques under the watchful eye of a good instructor. Make sure that you have both the skills and the gear to be able to take care of yourself when you go paddling.

Trip Planning: Playing the "What If" Game

Trip planning should start at your kitchen table long before your planned launch. You'll want to look carefully at a chart of your proposed paddling area and note spots that might be good places to duck behind for protection from a particular wind direction or simply to catch your breath and make any needed equipment adjustments. A guidebook like this can point you in the right direction and give you a general itinerary, but only you know what you're ready for on any given day. Monitor local weather reports for several days before your planned trip to get a feel for developing conditions. Then play the "What If" game.

What if the wind turns and blows hard out of the northwest instead of the expected southwest sea breeze? What if that cold front comes roaring through a few hours earlier than expected? What if fog creeps in to cover the channel you just crossed as you head for your island picnic? What if your youngest gets seasick and needs to settle an unruly stomach? It's a lot easier to solve anticipated problems in the comfort of your home than when looking over your shoulder at an unexpected squall line or approaching fog bank.

The Coast of Maine

Many a chagrined kayaker has found that local weather conditions don't always match the report on the weather radio. It's not uncommon to poke your nose out of the protection of a harbor and find that the actual wind direction is quite different from what your weather radio forecast just moments before your launch. In addition, things like headlands, river mouths, and even the wake from a passing ferry can alter expected conditions and wreak havoc with your plans.

As you play the "What If" game, make brief notes of your solutions to anticipated problems. Use a grease pencil on a chart case to note bearings to and from landmarks or navigational aids like buoys and day beacons. Or make notes in pencil on index cards that you can tuck into a pocket or inside a chart case. Make sure to record all the bearings you could possibly need, including the back bearings. Plotting a course while under way in a sea kayak isn't the easiest thing to do when the weather begins kicking up or you're tired and cold. Even the simple arithmetic of calculating a back, or return, bearing can be challenging if you're rattled. Remember to take your bearings over small distances so you'll have lots of checkpoints for staying found along the way and an early sense of what the wind and tidal current might be doing to your plans. Your chart case might end up looking like a strategic battle plan with all the circles, arrows, and notes you make, but you'll be able to trot out Plan B or even Plan C or D if needed. Knowing your options prior to launching will buy you some real peace of mind so you can enjoy each and every outing.

Weather Along the Coast

While Maine weather has always been considered fickle and its shifts often dramatic, there are some basic patterns that emerge during the summer months. The prevailing winds are southwesterly and will typically clock in at between 10 and 15 knots. Over the course of several days, cloud cover may thicken and bring rain before being driven off by a cold front that leaves behind the cooler, drier air that comes from the north and northwest. Winds on the back side of a cold front can be gusty and strong, and since they represent an offshore breeze, they should figure prominently in your trip planning. Winds from the southeast or east usually mean you're in for some crummy weather: rain, drizzle, and fog.

In addition to these general patterns, you have the local coastal conditions created by the warming and cooling of the land, along with the winds this creates. On a typical summer day, you can set your watch by the onshore breeze that begins to develop around 10:30 A.M. This wind from the south-southwest will gradually build throughout the middle of the day and early afternoon before retiring as the land begins to cool around sunset. You may experience a gentle land, or offshore, breeze in the early-evening hours and during the morning hours before the land has warmed enough to start the cycle anew. These cycles will be overridden by weather fronts that move through an area, but they should figure in your trip plans. It's always nice to have that southwest wind at your back for the return leg home.

Fog is a reality you will have to contend with during the paddling season in Maine. The warm southwesterly air that flows across the cool waters of the Gulf of Maine sets up this phenomenon, called advection fog. Dense fog banks may sit offshore and be pushed into the coastal waters by a southeast breeze, sometimes remaining for days at a time. Some areas of the Maine coast, like Petit Manan, see an average of 75 days of fog a year, most concentrated in late June through August. Anyone paddling Maine waters during the summer months will have to contend with fog at some point. Sleep late, read a good book, or head out for a hike on an inland trail. The fog will eventually blow away and always keep you guessing about its return.

Low-Impact Techniques for Kayakers

The islands off the coast of Maine may look rugged, but they are remarkably fragile. Their soil is often only a thin layer of matter that's slow to break down wastes and easily destroyed if it's repeatedly compacted over time. For this reason, try to walk only along the rocky shorelines or on established trails when you visit an island. You'll need to pack out all garbage and your own wastes and dispose of them on the mainland. Pack along some zipper-locking bags for discarded tissue, and deposit your wastes in a lined ammo can, Tupperware container, or commercial portable toilet (these methods work well and the state's outfitters have been practicing them for years).

The maps in this book indicate areas where camping is allowed. These sites may range from developed mainland campgrounds to remote and primitive island sites.

Except in designated areas, you will not be able to build fires on Maine's islands. It would be too easy for fire to spread to the many blowdowns and dry tinder found on these islands, and firetrucks don't run well offshore. Pack along a campstove for your lobster bake or mussel feed and you'll leave behind a prettier, safer island.

One of the joys of paddling the coast of Maine is watching all the creatures that make this their home, if only for the summer months. Many species breed and raise their young along Maine's coast and on the islands. Numerous islands are protected during the nesting season, and Maine's seal population is closely monitored. If a nesting bird or mother seal is disturbed and leaves her young, even for a short period of time, it can lessen the chances of the young's survival. We have seen young eiders separated from their mother by unaware kayakers who were enjoying paddling among these seabirds in an island cove. Gulls swooped in and killed three of the young before the kayakers got the message and retreated. It was a tragedy that could have been prevented with a good pair of binoculars and a willingness to observe wildlife without intruding.

Watching seals cavort around a half-tide ledge is a lot of fun; we've thoroughly enjoyed these observations over the years. It's less fun to paddle right up to a seal haul-out and then watch the animals dive for the cover of water and swim out of sight, yet we've seen kayakers do this. If you sit quietly away from the ledges, you can watch their natural behaviors as they stretch in the sun, doze, and nuzzle their offspring. Seal pups are especially sensitive to disturbances and need to remain on haul-outs and close to their mothers. If a kayaker flushes a group of seals from their haul-out, a pup may become separated from its mother or be stressed and less likely to survive this critical stage in its life. Seal pupping season occurs from late April through mid-June on the coast of Maine.

Sea kayaks are such wonderful, low-impact vessels for exploring the coast of Maine. We are quiet, leave no sheen of oil in our wake, and travel under our own power. By understanding the fragility of the landscapes we visit and the wildlife we observe, we can continue to protect these resources. There are too many magical places to explore and natural sights to see to let these things slip away. Please be careful and thoughtful as you explore the waters and islands of Maine.

Maine Island Trail

This 325-mile-long waterway is a trail designed for small-boaters that includes many overnight camping opportunities on coastal islands. The trail begins in Casco Bay and winds its way to Machias Bay through myriad seascapes with both public and private island access. This is not a developed trail with a clearly delineated start and finish, but rather a variety of island and mainland access points that allows you to travel a route by small boat and explore Maine's coastal environment.

The trail is managed by the nonprofit Maine Island Trail Association (MITA), whose members serve as stewards of the islands and monitor use of these sites. There are approximately eighty islands (it changes from year to year) accessible to MITA members, with about half being privately owned and the remainder under state ownership. MITA is a unique and useful organization that warrants your support if Maine's islands are to remain accessible and protected for years to come.

MITA encourages and sets standards for the use of low-impact techniques on Maine's islands. MITA is also in the process of determining the recreational carrying capacity for the islands on the trail and posts voluntary guidelines for overnight camping limits. Members may volunteer in an Adopt-an-Island program, take part in work parties that keep island shores and campsites clean, or informally serve as additional eyes and ears out on the trail during the boating season. One of the membership privileges is a guidebook that details low-impact techniques and island access points. No commercially available guidebook could, or should, ever replace this invaluable resource. For more information on MITA:

41A Union Wharf, Portland, ME 04101; 207–761–8225; mita@ime.net

P.O. Box C, Rockland, ME 04841; 207–596–6456; islands@ime.net

www.mita.org

MITA's Mission Statement: **The Maine Island Trail Association's goal is to establish a model of thoughtful use and volunteer stewardship for the Maine islands that will assure their conservation in a natural state while providing an exceptional recreational asset that is maintained and cared for by the people who use it.**

About This Book

The most difficult thing about paddling in Maine is narrowing the choices to a manageable number. Each trip in this guidebook offers options and alternate routes for particular wind and tide concerns. If we have offered too many options, it is only to whet your paddling imagination. The coast of Maine provides endless sea kayaking enjoyment across a wide range of outings. In almost every instance you may find ways to shorten a recommended trip if you're forced to fit things into a harried schedule or the weather doesn't cooperate. You will always be able to lengthen a given trip; we have been known to linger at a single tidal pool for hours, content to watch invertebrates—at *their* pace.

Unlike white-water trips, sea kayaking outings cannot be clearly assigned a class of difficulty. Wind, weather, tidal currents, and even storms far out at sea may change any outing on a given day and even at a given hour. We have tried to point out concerns and nudge you into considering your options. Reviewing your chart with weather forecasts and tide tables in mind will help you plan for the best and safest outing possible.

The small maps provided for each trip in this book are not meant to be used for navigational purposes. They do not show navigational aids unless specifically mentioned in the text. They are provided to give you a quick glance at the location of a given trip and its general features. Once you decide on a particular trip, refer to the NOAA chart number provided. These nautical charts may be purchased at marine chandleries, outfitters' stores, and other places that sell boating supplies. Almost all of the trips refer to NOAA charts that use a scale of 1:40,000 (the one exception is the map for Route 17: St. George River from Warren to Thomaston).

This book begins with trips in the Portland area and continues with outings downeast. While we don't hold to the notion that there is nothing south of Portland worth exploring, we felt that there were good reasons for choosing Casco Bay to mark our southernmost point. The geology of Maine's coast changes dramatically in the Portland area. Southwest of Portland there are broad expanses of beach and a gradually curving coastline; northeast of the city the coastline becomes more ragged and islands more common. The abundance of islands and the fascinating complexity of coastline are two key factors that make Maine a favorite sea kayaking destination.

This book is primarily about day trips by sea kayak. While we offer several overnight possibilities, our focus is on day paddling from publicly accessible launch sites along the coast. You may find that you can string together several day trips with the lodging options or even island camping sites available along the way. Part of the fun in exploring is to think creatively about your own options and what you'd like to gain from an outing. For this reason, we have kept our format flexible and our minds open. So should you!

Portland
to Freeport

Route 1

--- ➤

Jewell Island

This is a destination paddle to the shores of Jewell Island, a popular public island about 8 miles out from Portland launch sites. There is lots to explore on this impressive island with its observation towers, old gun emplacements, and hiking trails. Jewell Island has served as a fortified site guarding the approaches to and from Casco Bay over several centuries. Exploring Jewell Island is a far cry from a wilderness experience. A typical summer day's visit may mean landing among rafts of powerboaters lugging large coolers and grills ashore for a weekend party, and the anchorages along the northwest shore are usually crowded with small sailboats and yachts. But a visit in the off-season or during midweek can be quite nice, and there is plenty of room to spread out and roam.

Jewell Island is also open for overnight visits (camping during a summer weekend can be a complete madhouse) and has several campsites, fire pits, and pit toilets. A lot of the credit for keeping Jewell clean and well maintained goes to local volunteers and MITA members, who have worked hard over the years to keep this island healthy and accessible to a diverse group of people.

The paddle out to Jewell Island requires decent weather, because you're a bit far out for a quick return to the mainland. You'll need to contend with a lot of boat traffic. Be particularly aware of commercial traffic: both large vessels plying the restricted shipping channels and the ferry service. The main shipping channels can be determined from the chart, and kayakers should steer clear

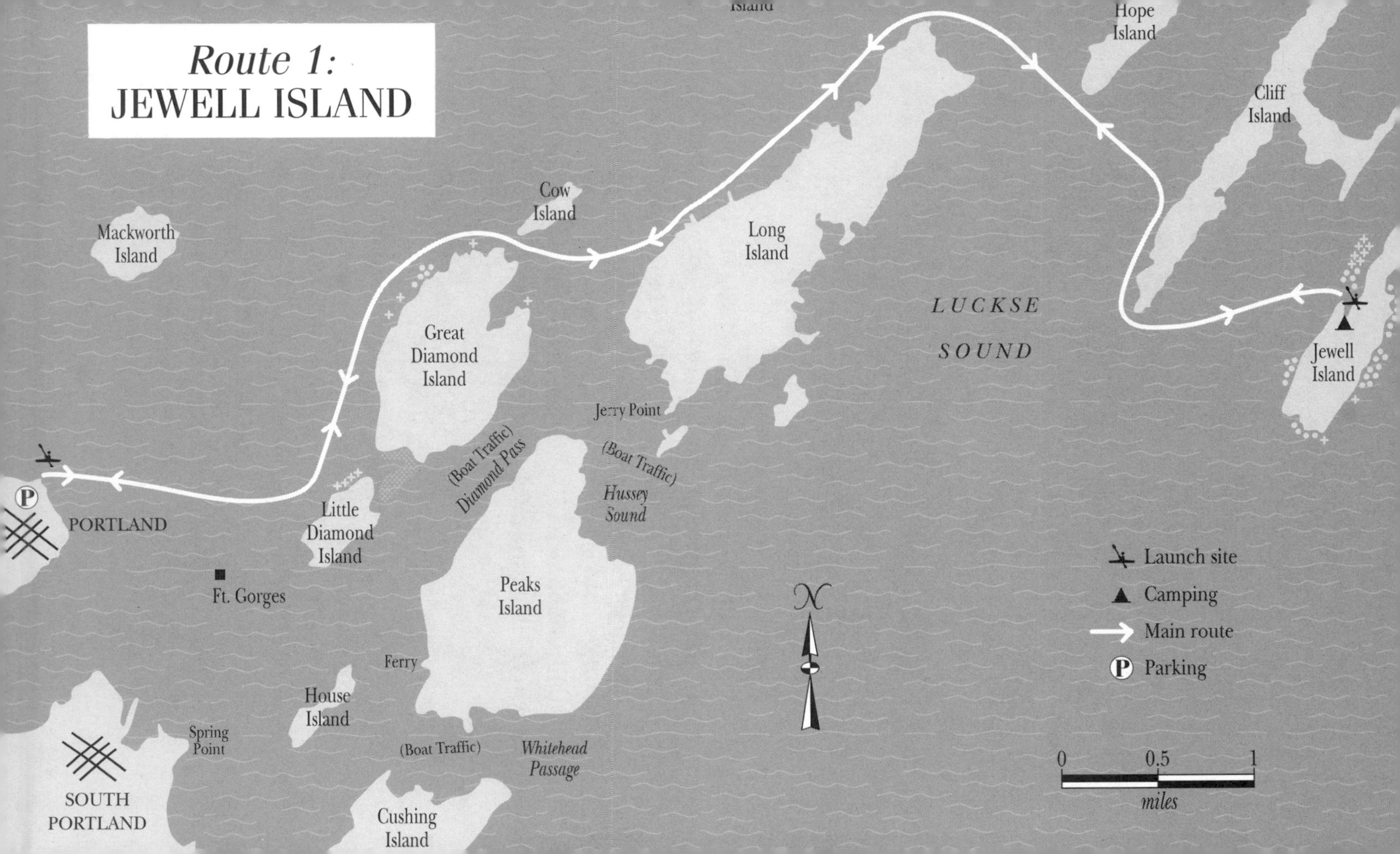

Route 1:
JEWELL ISLAND

Legend

✈ Launch site
▲ Camping
⬆ Main route
Ⓟ Parking

Jewell Island

Cliff Island

Hope Island

Island

LUCKSE SOUND

Long Island

Cow Island

Jerry Point

(Boat Traffic)

Hussey Sound

Peaks Island

Whitehead Passage

Great Diamond Island

(Boat Traffic) Diamond Pass

Ferry

(Boat Traffic)

Cushing Island

Little Diamond Island

House Island

Ft. Gorges

Mackworth Island

Spring Point

PORTLAND

SOUTH PORTLAND

miles
0   0.5   1

of them at all times. If you must cross a shipping channel, do so at a right angle and only when you are certain you have clear space to cross safely. If you must wait for traffic to clear, so be it. Do not pick your way across and expect others to adjust to your presence. Larger vessels may not have the ability to maneuver, and their deep drafts place limits on where they can travel. As a small-boater, always assume that you cannot be seen and proceed accordingly.

Even though there are shorter routes to Jewell Island, plan on paddling a route that will minimize your exposure to the shipping traffic moving into and out of Portland. Most of this traffic moves along the main shipping lanes between Portland Head and Cushing Island. By staying north of Fort Gorges and to the north and northwest of Little and Great Diamond Islands, you will miss the largest ships—and they will miss you. Diamond Pass is particularly busy, so you'd do well to avoid this, instead shooting across to Long Island and rounding its northern end. From there you can hop across to Cliff Island and then on to Jewell Island. Not only does this route keep you out of some busy shipping lanes, but it also gives you some protection from southerly or southwesterly breezes for most of the way.

TRIP HIGHLIGHTS: Vessels of every stripe can be observed as you pick your way through the busy harbor. Exploring Jewell Island is a rollicking time.

TRIP DURATION/LENGTH: The round trip paddle to Jewell Island and back is at least 16 miles, so you'll need to make an early start unless you're planning to camp overnight. If you encounter any rough water or troubling winds, you can cut this trip short at any point with a chance to regroup on Little Chebeague or Fort Gorges.

NAVIGATIONAL AIDS: NOAA Chart 13290 Casco Bay (scale 1:40,000). This entire route is well marked with buoys, many with light and sound characteristics. You'll pass as many as sixteen

different buoys along this route. As you cross from Cow Island to Long Island, note the lighted buoy as well as the one off the northern point of Long Island. Lighted bell buoy off Hope Island and Johns Ledge buoy off Cliff Island.

CAUTIONS: Lots of commercial and pleasure boat traffic from just about every direction.

LAUNCH SITE: There is a nice launch site at the Eastern Promenade with a fine view of Casco Bay from the top of the hill. You can drop off your gear close to the water before parking in the large lot on the site. Either use the recreational boat ramp (there's a fee) or launch from the small beach beyond the bathrooms. To find the Eastern Promenade, take exit 8 (Washington Street), turn left onto Eastern Promenade, and drive for a bit less than a mile before turning left onto Cutter Street. Stay on Cutter past the large parking lot and head toward the water.

LOCAL ATTRACTIONS: The Portland Public Market (207–288–2000), downtown at the intersection of Preble Street and Cumberland Avenue, is a wonderful place to load up on all the makings for a fine picnic lunch. Chase Leavitt (207–772–3751), on Dana Street in the Old Port, has a great selection of nautical books, charts, and instruments. It is also fun to ride the ferry service that accesses the communities on islands around Casco Bay. The Casco Bay Lines (207–774–7871) ferry terminal is on Commercial Street. And of course, Portland is full of options for lodging, eating, and shopping. For more information, contact the Portland Visitors Information Center, 305 Commercial Street, Portland, ME 04101; 207–772–5800; www.visitportland.com.

Route 2

Exploring Portland Harbor

After our previous warnings about Portland Harbor boat traffic (see Route 1), it may seem odd to suggest a trip exploring these waters. However, we will suggest routes that will keep you out of the major shipping lanes. The paddling in this area is well protected and generally calm— except for any jangled nerves on your part. The Eastern Promenade launch site is your best bet, since it keeps you to the north of big boats and allows for side trips to Back Cove and beyond.

One of the most interesting sites to visit is Fort Gorges, which sits just over a mile from the Eastern Promenade. The fascinating remains of this fort, construction of which was begun in 1848, are owned by the city of Portland, and the site is open during daylight hours. There is little to the island other than the fort, which sprawls over the ledges that are part of its foundation. You'll find a small beach and wharf on the northern side by the entrance to the fort.

The design features of Fort Gorges are surprisingly elegant, with stone arches and an interior courtyard where you can imagine the sounds of troops preparing for battle. However, Fort Gorges has never actually been used to any real degree, though it was manned following its completion in 1864. There was less concern at the time for invasion from the Confederates than about problems from Confederate allies like the British. The fort's strategic location certainly would have meant trouble to any gunboats trying to sneak into Portland Harbor. Please be careful as you explore—there's a lot of loose stone and brick. Wooden walkways span some sections.

From the Eastern Promenade you also have easy access to Back Cove, which is a shallow piece of water better known for the path that encircles it. This is a favorite jogging, walking, and in-line skating path that sees constant foot traffic. Back Cove is clearly visible from I–295, and while it isn't a quiet paddle, it's an interesting one if you like urban paddle trips. You'll be heading west around East End and under the railroad bridge and then the I–295 bridge. Take a deep breath as you pass the B & M Beans factory on the northern shore—you really can smell the beans cooking! Back Cove is very shallow and dries at low tide, so you'll need a half tide or better to explore. Plenty of gulls and cormorants hang out here; the area is actually a preserve managed by the state.

TRIP HIGHLIGHTS: Exploring Fort Gorges and watching the traffic pile up as you watch the shorebirds in Back Cove.

TRIP DURATION/LENGTH: The paddle out to Fort Gorges and back is a bit less than 2.5 miles. Approach the island from the north to stay well away from shipping lanes. You can continue from here to the north along the shores of the two Diamond Islands or even to Little Chebeague Island. From Eastern Promenade to Back Cove is a round trip of just over 4.5 miles.

NAVIGATIONAL AIDS: Chart 13290 Casco Bay (1:40,000) and Chart 13292 Portland Harbor (1:20,000). Light at Diamond Island Ledge off Fort Gorges. Red nun at the railroad bridge as you approach Back Cove.

CAUTIONS: Commercial and pleasure boat traffic, especially as you head out to Fort Gorges. Be careful of water levels in Back Cove on an ebbing tide.

LAUNCH SITE: There is a good launch site at Eastern Promenade with a fine view of Casco Bay from the top of the hill. Drop off your gear close to the water before parking in the large lot on the side. You can use the recreational boat ramp (there's a fee) or launch

Portland Harbor

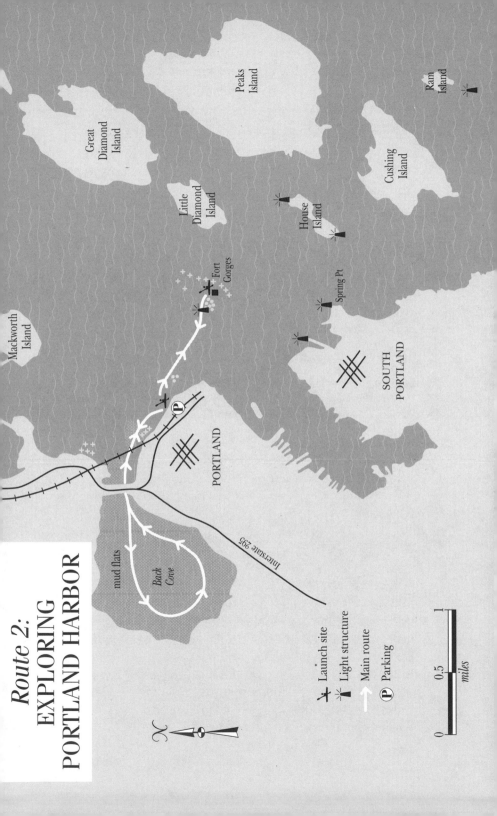

Route 2:
EXPLORING
PORTLAND HARBOR

Ram Island

Peaks Island

Great Diamond Island

Cushing Island

Little Diamond Island

House Island

Fort Gorges

Mackworth Island

Spring Pt

SOUTH PORTLAND

PORTLAND

Interstate 295

mud flats

Back Cove

Launch site
Light structure
Main route
Parking

0   0.5   1
miles

from the small beach beyond the bathrooms. To find the Eastern Promenade, take exit 8 (Washington Street), turn left onto Eastern Promenade, and drive for a bit less than a mile before turning left onto Cutter Street. Follow this past the large parking lot and toward the water.

LOCAL ATTRACTIONS: Watch the pedestrian traffic circle you as you sit in Back Cove. The Portland Public Market (207–288–2000), downtown at the intersection of Preble Street and Cumberland Avenue, is a wonderful place to load up on all the makings for a fine picnic lunch. Chase Leavitt (207–772–3751), on Dana Street in the Old Port, has a great selection of nautical books, charts, and instruments. It is also fun to ride the ferry service that accesses the communities on the islands around Casco Bay. The Casco Bay Lines (207–774–7871) ferry terminal is on Commercial Street. And of course, Portland is full of options for lodging, eating, and shopping. (See Route 1: Jewell Island for how to contact the Portland Visitors Information Center.)

Portland Harbor

Route 3

Cousins Island

It is always a pleasant surprise when you can find quiet
places to explore close to a large population center. As you
listen to the sounds of traffic recede with each paddle
stroke, you can't help but feel a bit lucky to leave all that
hustle and bustle behind. Exploring around Cousins Island
and the salt marshes that sit off its northern shore makes for
some quiet bird-watching. At low tide only kayaks and
canoes can poke among these grasses; large swaths of water
are less than 2 feet deep, and many a motorboat prop has
tangled in these grasses and stuck fast in the thick mud.
Don't even think of getting out of your boat or you will, too.

As you depart from the Yarmouth town landing, you'll
paddle along a well marked channel of the Royal River for
about a mile. This is a no-wake zone for the many
powerboaters and fishermen who use this launch site, and
at low tide the channel narrows considerably; stay well to the
side so they can pass. As you paddle between Browns Point
and Parker Point at the mouth of Royal River, you'll see the
entrance to the Cousins River off to your left. This is a nice
stretch of water that you can explore, but only on the upper
half of the tide. The sounds of traffic will gradually increase
as you near the interstate. Still, you will likely see great blue
herons, snowy egrets, and red-winged blackbirds. It is easy to
sit and enjoy a snack or hone your bird-watching skills in
these protected waters.

The nice loop trip around Cousins and Littlejohn
Islands can be expanded to include a stop on Little
Chebeague Island or Basket Island. Little Chebeague Island,

a popular public island that sits off the southwestern end of Great Chebeague Island, has several sand and gravel beaches for landing. Its interior features 2 miles of trails that explore the remains of old cottages and a hotel. Little Chebeague Island is known for its ticks, nettles, browntail moth caterpillars, and poison ivy, so move carefully. Basket Island, which is managed by a local land trust, has a nice gravel bar for landing on the east shore at low tide; its northeast point allows easy access as well. There are walking trails on this nine-acre island, and you are likely to have company from fellow kayakers and powerboaters. Keep an eye out for poison ivy on these shores as well.

Kayakers are often spoiled about water depths when it comes to reading a chart. If it isn't green and it isn't low tide, then we figure we're okay. Some of the areas on this trip will force you to actually read the soundings if you are paddling at low tide, especially during a full or new moon. As you swing around Cousins Island to the north, be very careful about picking your way through at low tide. Small runs of water allow you to navigate through the grassy areas, but often only a skim of water sits over thick mud, so beware. There are two approaches to the Royal River: one from the southeast and one from the southwest. As a kayaker, you have more options, but only if you pay attention.

TRIP HIGHLIGHTS: A very accessible piece of water that is pleasantly quiet and great for novice paddlers. Shorebirds are numerous on the mud flats.

TRIP DURATION/LENGTH: A loop from Yarmouth around the islands of Cousins and Littlejohn covers about 10.5 miles; including Little Chebeague Island in your travels adds 3 miles. To include Basket Island in the Cousins Island loop, swing wide to the southwest to add another 1.5 miles. A lazy exploration of the Cousins River will cover 4 to 5 miles round trip.

Cousins Island

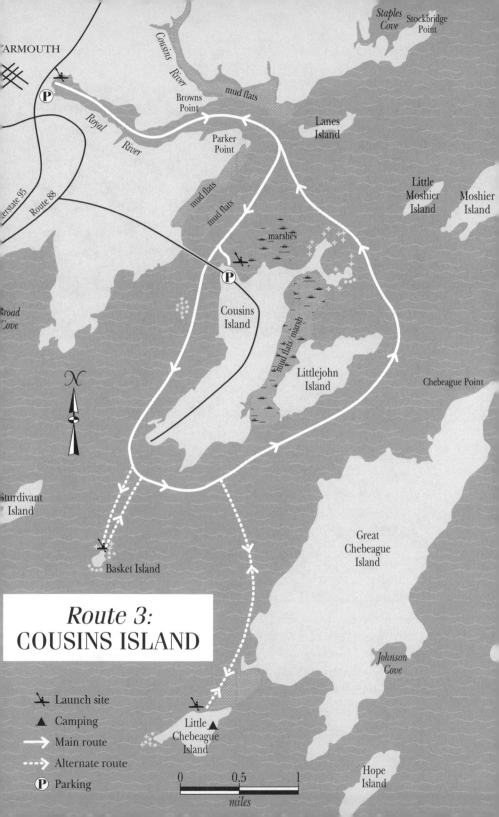

YARMOUTH

Staples Cove

Stockbridge Point

Cousins River

Browns Point

mud flats

Parker Point

Royal River

Interstate 95

Route 88

mud flats

mud flats

mud flats marsh

Lanes Island

Little Moshier Island

Moshier Island

marshes

Broad Cove

Cousins Island

Littlejohn Island

Chebeague Point

Sturdivant Island

Great Chebeague Island

Basket Island

Johnson Cove

Route 3: COUSINS ISLAND

Little Chebeague Island

Hope Island

Legend

- ⚓ Launch site
- ▲ Camping
- → Main route
- ⇢ Alternate route
- Ⓟ Parking

0   0.5   1

miles

NAVIGATIONAL AIDS: Chart 13290 Casco Bay (1:40,000). Lighted buoy at entrance of Royal River channel. Lighted buoy off Basket Island and marking the crossing to Little Chebeague Island.

CAUTIONS: Mud flats that can constrict boat traffic to a single track adventure.

LAUNCH SITE: To reach the Yarmouth town landing, take exit 17 off I–95 and turn right onto Route 1 south. Be ready to take the first left onto Route 88. Follow Route 88 for 0.2 miles and turn left onto Bayview Road. Take the first right off Bayview Road; this is Old Shipyard Road. The landing is 0.5 miles further. There is a harbormaster's office (where you'll need to pay the $10 nonresident town fee), a pay phone, and a portable toilet. A large parking area is available to recreational boaters, but it will fill up on a busy summer weekend. You could also use the launch site on Sandy Point on Cousins Island. Turn left into Sandy Point Park just after coming off the bridge to Cousins Island. You can hand-carry your kayak to the water, but you may have trouble accessing open water except on the upper half of the tide.

LOCAL ATTRACTIONS: It is a short hop to Portland, which has all the services you'd expect in a city. (See Route 1: Jewell Island for how to contact the Portland Visitors Information Center.)

Route 4

Harraseeket River and Maquoit Bay

These waters are amazingly quiet, because the abundant mudflats and shallow areas are not inviting to many other boaters. However, it does serve as an invitation to a wide variety of birds that feed among the shallows and use Maquoit Bay as a resting stop for spring and fall migrations. In the summer months you can see blue herons and snowy egrets, which congregate on the mudflats to feed. Until May, waterfowl abound: Pintails, teal, mallards, and widgeons can be found, sometimes in sizable numbers. In the fall you can watch for migrant hawks like kestrels, northern harriers, merlins, and sharp-shinned hawks.

Just below Maquoit Bay you'll find the undeveloped shores of Wolf Neck, where there is a 218-acre state park with hiking trails, natural history displays, picnic tables, and bathroom facilities. It is not easy to land on the rocky shores of the park and there are no facilities for boaters, so do not count on making a landing here. (For the record, the park's name is Wolfe's Neck Woods State Park, named for an early settler, Henry Wolfe.)

The shallow waters in this area also make launching a matter of timing. All the launch sites require half tide or better, except the Yarmouth town landing, which puts you farthest away from upper Maquoit Bay and will cut into your meandering. Freeport's Winslow Memorial Park is a good bet, because you can push your timing a bit and even launch close to low tide by picking your way among rocks and mud. You'll get your feet muddy, but you won't necessarily lose your footwear.

Exploring down the Harraseeket River is a pleasant paddle. On the top third of the tide, it is fun to explore the fingers of water in the direction of Mast Landing as the river meanders its way inland. This portion of the river is completely dry at low tide, so don't be tempted to push things; plan this trip on a rising tide to be safe. The area is serene and restful and, while there is a boatyard and marina in South Freeport, these waters are quiet and calm. The tidal current is not strong and allows for some lazy exploring.

TRIP HIGHLIGHTS: Serenity, shorebirds, and a pleasantly undeveloped shoreline along Wolf Neck.

TRIP DURATION/LENGTH: A swing up through Maquoit Bay is about 10 to 11 miles from either Recompense Shores Campground or Winslow Memorial Park. Both of these sites allow for exploring the Harraseeket River, a round trip of 7 to 8 miles.

NAVIGATIONAL AIDS: Chart 13290 Casco Bay (1:40,000). Lighted buoy at entrance to Harraseeket River.

CAUTIONS: You must not push your luck on the ebbing tide, especially in the upper reaches of the Harraseeket River or upper Maquoit Bay.

LAUNCH SITE: The Recompense Shores Campground allows kayakers to launch from its property. You'll need the upper half of the tide to do so. There is limited parking at this pleasant site, where you launch adjacent to the bridge. Bow Street is the road directly across from L. L. Bean in Freeport (everybody knows where that is). Follow Bow Street for 1.5 miles and take a right onto Flying Point Road. Follow this for 0.8 miles, turn right onto Wolf Neck Road, and continue for 1.7 miles until you turn onto Burnett Road (you'll see signs for the campground). Go just beyond the campground to the bridge.

Winslow Memorial Park is a recreation area run by the town of Freeport with a swimming beach, picnic tables, and a concrete boat ramp that is good for all but two hours on either side of low tide, though you may push this a bit. There is a $2.00 parking fee.

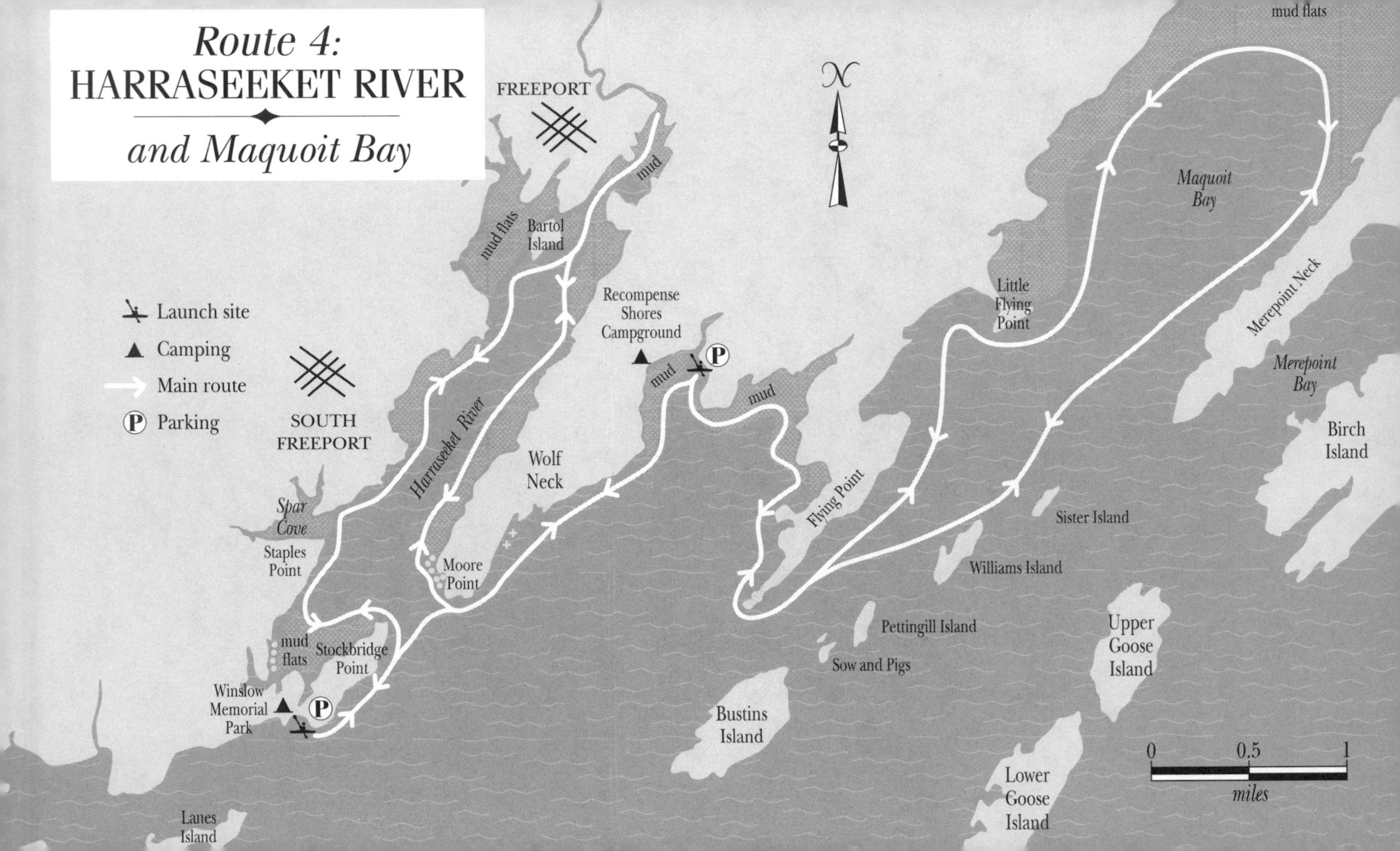

Route 4:
HARRASEEKET RIVER
◆
and Maquoit Bay

Legend:
- ⤬ Launch site
- ▲ Camping
- ⬆ Main route
- Ⓟ Parking

mud flats

FREEPORT

Bartol Island

mud flats

mud

SOUTH
FREEPORT

Spar
Cove
Staples
Point

Harraseeket River

Moore
Point

Wolf
Neck

Recompense
Shores
Campground

Ⓟ

mud

mud

Flying Point

Little
Flying
Point

Maquoit Bay

Merepoint Neck

Merepoint
Bay

Birch
Island

Sister Island

Williams Island

Pettingill Island

Sow and Pigs

Upper
Goose
Island

Lower
Goose
Island

Bustins
Island

Stockbridge
Point

mud
flats

Ⓟ

Winslow
Memorial
Park

Lanes
Island

Scale:
0   0.5   1
miles

Take exit 19 (Desert Road) off I–95, then head south on Route 1 for 2.0 miles and turn left onto South Freeport Road. Follow this for 0.5 mile, taking the second right onto Staples Point Road. Follow this road 1.6 miles to Winslow Memorial Park.

LOCAL ATTRACTIONS: Wolfe's Neck Woods State Park is a great place to visit; there's much to learn from viewing its displays and walking its trails. The Wolfe's Neck Farm, a nonprofit demonstration farm, is also close by. It sells organic beef and vegetables and is open to visitors. The town of Freeport has more shopping than anyone can fathom. At the end of Main Street in South Freeport, you'll find the Harraseeket, which serves fresh local seafood on picnic tables, the old-fashioned way.

In addition, you can camp at Winslow Memorial Park (207–865–4198) or at Recompense Shores Campground (207–865–9307).

Harraseeket River and Maquoit Bay

Brunswick *to* Boothbay

Route 5

Eagle Island (Casco Bay)

Eagle Island was once the summer home of Arctic explorer Admiral Robert Peary. It is now a historic site maintained by the state and open to the public during daylight hours. There is a cottage furnished much the way it was during Peary's residence with some of the family's personal belongings on display. It was here that his wife, Josephine, received his telegram on September 6, 1909, stating that he had reached the North Pole.

The island is a beautiful one, with gravel and sand pocket beaches for easy landing and a saltwater pool on its north end that is replenished and scoured clean with each tidal cycle. The state has built a large pier and placed moorings for larger boats; kayaks can land to the south of the pier or on the pocket beach just below the cottage's stone foundation. There is a fee of $2.00 per person for visitors, but you may stay and explore as much as you like from sunrise to sunset. You'll find a long expanse of lawn for stretching out in the sun and plenty of exposed ledge for picnics. Several trails crisscross this seventeen-acre island.

The paddle out to Eagle is a straightforward two miles from Basin Point, though you'll need to be ever vigilant of other boat traffic, which zooms at you from every direction. The confusion of so many boat wakes can actually make this a bumpy ride out, and a wind-tide opposition can worsen things as well. There are numerous shoals around Eagle that produce ledge breaks, but these are easily skirted by kayaks. A circumnavigation of Eagle Island may expose you to some rough paddling on the south side, but is certainly worth checking out if you feel inclined.

As you paddle out from Basin Point, you can aim for Upper Flag Island, which offers some nice protection from a southwesterly breeze. The low cliffs along the western side are very pretty. It is clear that locals use this island on a regular basis for picnics on the beaches on both the southern and northern sides. After you round the western point of Upper Flag Island, Eagle Island will pop into view, with its cottage perched on the bluff and the pier on its western side. A short stretch of water between Upper Flag and Eagle produces some confusion as currents cross each other, but you can steam your way through this quickly.

Jewell Island (see Route 1) sits just 2 miles to the southwest, but this route to Jewell can be very exposed; also, the cluster of ledges between Eagle and Jewell can really kick up and create some challenging conditions. There can be significant currents in Broad Sound as you set off from Eagle Island toward Jewell, so be aware of the tide tables for this area. This crossing is not recommended except under

Eagle Island (Casco Bay)

calm conditions. It should never be undertaken in a strong offshore wind. Instead, consider extending your paddle by exploring up into Potts Harbor, where you can land on tiny Bar Island, though low tide is a bit of a challenge.

TRIP HIGHLIGHTS: Exploring Eagle Island and the summer home of Admiral Robert Peary.

TRIP DURATION/LENGTH: The paddle out to Eagle Island from Dolphin Marine on Basin Point is less than 2 miles, but you'll want to save plenty of time to explore Eagle Island and can certainly make this a full-day trip. Side trips include explorations around Eagle Island and across to Haskell Island and into Potts Harbor to Bar Island, which can stretch your paddling mileage to 6 or more miles if you feel the need.

NAVIGATIONAL AIDS: Chart 13290 Casco Bay (1:40,000). Bell buoy off Little Birch Island; nun buoy west of Flag Island; nun buoy off SW point of Eagle Island.

Eagle Island (Casco Bay)

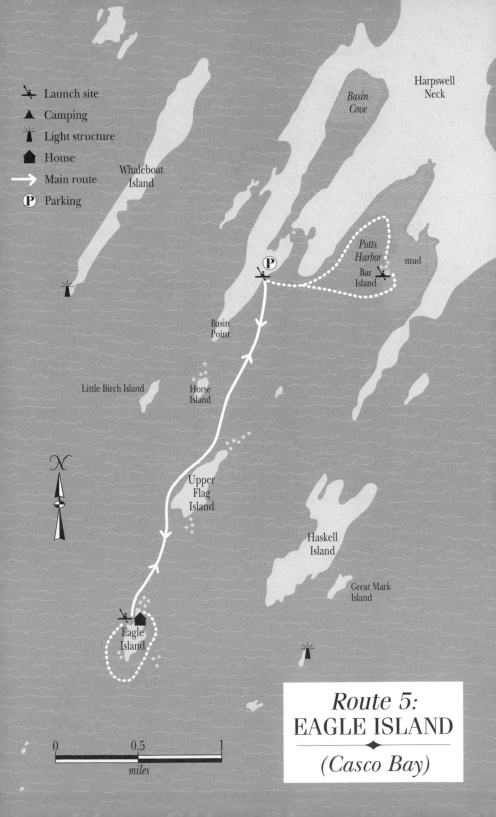

Legend

- ✈ Launch site
- ▲ Camping
- ⚑ Light structure
- ⌂ House
- → Main route
- Ⓟ Parking

Harpswell
Neck

Basin
Cove

Whaleboat
Island

Potts
Harbor

Ⓟ

mud

Bar
Island

Basin
Point

Little Birch Island

Horse
Island

N

Upper
Flag
Island

Haskell
Island

Great Mark
Island

Eagle
Island

Route 5:
EAGLE ISLAND
◆
(Casco Bay)

0   0.5   1
miles

CAUTIONS: Boat traffic can create squirrely water, especially on the final approach to Eagle Island. Exposure to winds and open water on the southern side of Eagle Island can be challenging.

LAUNCH SITE: Dolphin Marine (207–833–6000) at Basin Point. There is a $5.00 fee for launching and $5.00 for parking. The boat ramp is all-tide and paved; there is also a small patch of gravel along the edge for kayaks. To reach Dolphin Marine from the south, take Route 123 from Brunswick down the Harpswell Peninsula. From the north you can take Route 24 and turn right onto Mountain Road to access Route 123. A little over 3.0 miles from Harpswell Center, turn right onto Ash Point Road. Proceed on Ash Point Road for 0.2 mile and turn right onto Basin Point Road. This road will take you around the basin and end at Dolphin Marine and Restaurant. There are also BLUE DOLPHIN MARINE signs at each of these turns.

LOCAL ATTRACTIONS: The Dolphin Restaurant serves local seafood and also has a snack counter with ice cream and milk shakes for a postpaddling treat. If you want to learn more about Robert Peary and fellow explorer Harold MacMillan, both Bowdoin alumni, visit the Peary-MacMillan Arctic Museum at nearby Bowdoin College in Brunswick (207–725–3416). There are plenty of lodging establishments on both the Harpswell Peninsula and Bailey and Orrs Islands. The Harpswell Inn (207–833–5509) is a few miles down from the put-in on Lookout Point Road; the Hazel-Bea House (207–725–6834) faces Quahog Bay on South Dyers Cove Road.

Paddling in Wind

Paddling in wind requires a strategy. Otherwise you're liable to spend way too much energy battling this element, which often seems intent on ruining your day. Paddling into a headwind can be the most tiring; conserve your energy with a lower-angled stroke that is shorter and has a quicker cadence than your "Sunday driving" action. Try to keep moving, and look for a piece of shoreline when you need a break. If you're feeling discouraged, look to the side to remind yourself that you really are moving forward. It will give you a boost.

Paddling in beam seas can actually be the most difficult, because you'll have to adjust your balance every time seas pass beneath your hull from the side, and you'll often have to work hard to keep your kayak on course. If you have a rudder or skeg on your boat, this might be the time to consider dropping it. Otherwise, adjust your weight by lifting your hip and knee on the downwind side. This subtle weight shift will help keep your boat from swinging into the wind and naturally cause a slight lean into the beam seas, which will help stabilize you as you paddle forward.

Paddling in following seas can be somewhat disconcerting but often means a free ride. As the wave passes beneath your hull, you'll accelerate down its face, only to slow and possibly wallow on its back side. Don't try to paddle up the back side; keep an easy cadence until the next wave lifts you. Pick up your pace as you accelerate and then slow again as the wave passes. If you need to make a course correction, you'll find it much easier to do so as you are lifted by the wave, since more of your boat is out of the water at this point.

Route 6

Sebascodegan Island and Quahog Bay

Quahog Bay is tucked into the center of Sebascodegan Island and appears to be cradled in the arms of this large and fascinating spot. You'll see plenty of sailboats that pull into the many protected anchorages in these waters. There are numerous small coves and fingers of water to explore throughout Quahog Bay, and you'll find yourself well protected from the wind.

If you choose to venture outside the protection of the upper part of the bay, there's some nice exploring around Yarmouth Island and the ledges that sit to the south. However, a sustained southerly or even the strong afternoon sea breezes from the southwest can really kick up the water around these ledges; they are best explored during quieter times. You can also access the New Meadows River by paddling through Ridley Cove and rounding Cundy Point (see New Meadows River, Route 7). Again, a strong southerly should warn you away from this exposed area.

Card Cove, which sits on the western side of Quahog Bay, is a great place to tuck into. You can travel well up into the northern finger of water before you have to turn around. If the conditions are reassuringly mild, you may want to continue around Gun Point to explore up into the picturesque Gun Point Cove on the southwest end of Sebascodegan Island. If the wind is a strong northwesterly or southerly breeze, this leg of the trip should not be undertaken. Instead, you should enjoy the more protected areas in upper Quahog Bay and Card Cove.

Little Snow Island is the small island that sits off the southeastern end of Snow Island in the upper bay and is open for day and overnight use. This makes a wonderful lunch spot, though you probably won't have it to yourself during the peak summer months. You'll likely see ospreys, eiders, and a variety of seabirds throughout this area and shorebirds feeding along the convoluted shoreline.

TRIP HIGHLIGHTS: Great scenery in protected waters as you watch the parade of sailboats that cruise the area.

TRIP DURATION/LENGTH: You can paddle as little or as much as your heart desires. It is a mere hop of less than a mile from Great Island Boat Yard to Little Snow Island, and only 1.5 miles if you use the launch site at Bethel Point Boat Yard to the south. Yet you'll find miles of exploring in this protected patch of water.

Sebascodegan Island and Quahog Bay

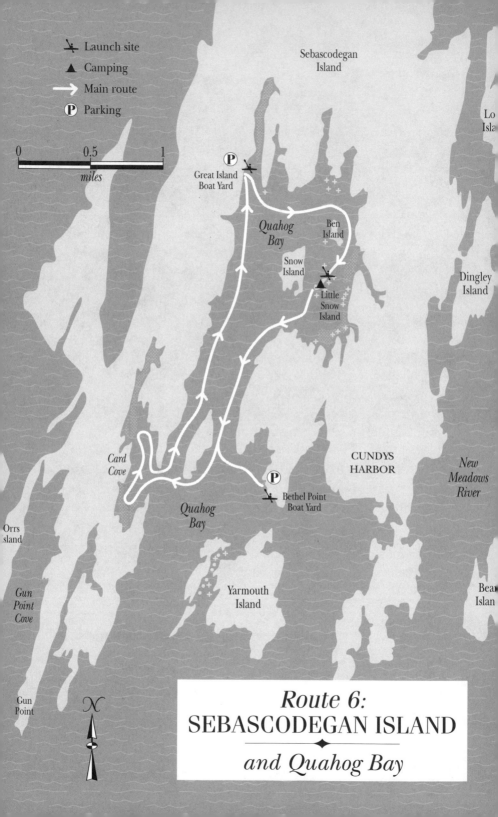

Launch site
▲ Camping
→ Main route
ⓅParking

0   0.5   1
miles

Sebascodegan
Island

Lo
Isla

Ⓟ
Great Island
Boat Yard

*Quahog
Bay*

Ben
Island

Snow
Island

Little
Snow
Island

Dingley
Island

*Card
Cove*

CUNDYS
HARBOR

*New
Meadows
River*

Ⓟ
Bethel Point
Boat Yard

*Quahog
Bay*

Orrs
.sland

*Gun
Point
Cove*

Yarmouth
Island

Bea
Islan

Gun
Point

N

Route 6:
SEBASCODEGAN ISLAND
◆
and Quahog Bay

NAVIGATIONAL AIDS: Chart 13290 Casco Bay (1:40,000). Nun buoy off Gun Point.

CAUTIONS: A strong southerly can funnel straight up lower Quahog Bay and Gun Point Cove.

LAUNCH SITE: The Great Island Boat Yard (207–729–1639) is on Route 24, 2.0 miles south of the Gurnet Strait bridge. There is a $5.00 fee for launching from its all-tide ramp which puts you into Orrs Cove on the northwest side of Quahog Bay. The Bethel Point Boat Yard is used for launching from the public boat ramp at Hen Cove. Parking at the ramp is by permit only for town residents, but you may launch from the ramp after parking at the adjacent Bethel Point Boat Yard. From Route 24 turn left onto Cundys Harbor Road after crossing the Gurnet Strait bridge. Follow this road for 3.2 miles and turn right onto Bethel Point Road before you come to the town of Cundys Harbor. Follow this road to its end at the boat ramp and turn into the boatyard on your right. There is a fee of $5.00 to park your car at the boatyard. If no one is around, go up the steps to the house on the hill; you should find a box to deposit your fee. There is a portable toilet available in the boatyard.

LOCAL ATTRACTIONS: Nearby Bailey Island has lodging and some wonderful seafood restaurants (they're all good), or you can relax at Bethel Point Bed and Breakfast (207–725–1115) or the Captain's Watch Bed and Breakfast (207–725–0979) and dine on fresh lobster at Holbook's Lobster Wharf and Grille in Cundys Harbor. The cribwork bridge which joins Orrs and Bailey Islands is a fascinating piece of work. It is constructed of large granite blocks which are stacked so that the strong tidal flow in this area can pour through them. At the southern end of Bailey Island is a statue dedicated to Maine fishermen and an impressive view across Casco Bay.

Route 7

New Meadows River

The New Meadows River flows along the eastern shores of Sebascodegan Island and offers plenty of paddling opportunities. The New Meadows is gentle unless severely constricted, as it is at Gurnet Strait and the entrance to the Basin. Gurnet Strait is best left alone except at slack tide—the current can fly through here at better than 7 knots during midtide. The entrance to The Basin is more reasonable and can be paddled during the entire tidal cycle, though at midtide you'll need an all-out sprint to push through an opposing tide. There are plenty of places to duck behind for protection from the wind throughout the run of the New Meadows, but because the river runs along a north–south axis, a strong southerly or southwesterly wind can funnel down its course and make for some tough going.

Indian Point Island, a tiny island spotted just to the west of Indian Point, is open to the public and makes a nice rest stop if needed. You may also choose to take a break by ducking into Back Cove behind Foster Point which sits across from Indian Point. The Audubon Society's Hamilton Sanctuary allows careful day use for a shore stop, but Back Cove is nearly dry at low tide. The Basin makes a fine destination, and the small island that sits at its southeast corner, Basin Island, is a Bureau of Parks and Lands island open to the public. You should confine your activities to the northern half of the island until August, since ospreys nest on the southern end. Please be careful of scrambling up from the beach; erosion is a constant problem for this island.

The Basin is a very popular hurricane hole for small-boaters and offers excellent protection and a quiet anchorage for the many pleasure boats that cruise these waters. The area to the south and west of Basin Island dries out or is only skimmed with water at low tide, so the best landing is on its eastern side. As you exit The Basin, you can look across the river and slightly south to Cundys Harbor, home to a sizable fishing fleet and boatyards.

There are plenty of nooks and crannies to explore on either side of the New Meadows River. Winnegance Bay is an open body of water just north of The Basin, or you can explore behind Long Island at half tide or better. If you use the Sawyer Park ramp, you'll see nearly the entire length of the New Meadows River during your paddle to The Basin and back. If you use the Brewer's Boat Yard put-in at Sebasco on the eastern shore, you can explore around privately owned Bear Island and Malaga Island before heading upriver towards the Basin. However, this launch site is limited to half tide or better and should not be pushed or you'll face a very muddy slog to and from the water.

TRIP HIGHLIGHTS: Unlimited gunkholing along this pastoral river with plenty of opportunities for bird-watching, picnics, and island visits.

TRIP DURATION/LENGTH: The round-trip paddle from Sawyer Park to The Basin and back is close to 16 miles, depending on how much you meander. This makes a great full-day trip unless you are

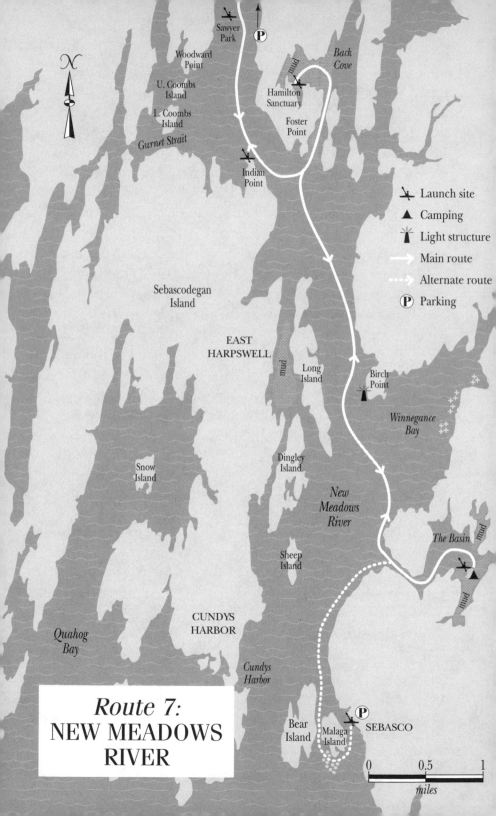

N

Sawyer
Park

Woodward
Point

U. Coombs
Island

L. Coombs
Island

Gurnet Strait

Indian
Point

mud

Back
Cove

Hamilton
Sanctuary

Foster
Point

⚓ Launch site

▲ Camping

☼ Light structure

→ Main route

⇢ Alternate route

Ⓟ Parking

Sebascodegan
Island

EAST
HARPSWELL

mud

Long
Island

Birch
Point

*Winnegance
Bay*

Snow
Island

Dingley
Island

*New
Meadows
River*

The Basin

mud

mud

Sheep
Island

CUNDYS
HARBOR

*Quahog
Bay*

*Cundys
Harbor*

Bear
Island

Malaga
Island

Ⓟ

SEBASCO

Route 7:
NEW MEADOWS
RIVER

0   0.5   1

miles

bucking any strong headwinds. With rest stops along the way, you can always cut this trip mileage to whatever feels comfortable. The shorter paddle to the Hamilton Sanctuary shore is only about 8 miles round trip from Sawyer Park.

NAVIGATIONAL AIDS: Chart 13290 Casco Bay (1:40,000). Day beacon at Bragdon Rock; Birch Point Light; Hen Ledge day beacon.

CAUTIONS: Gurnet Strait where the current can exceed 7 knots, strong winds that can funnel up or down the river's north–south axis.

LAUNCH SITE: Sawyer Park has an all-tide concrete boat ramp and pit toilet as well as ample parking. It is popular with powerboaters and sees plenty of use with its convenient location between Bath and Brunswick. You may choose to launch from Brewer's Boat Yard (207–389–1388) in Sebasco on the upper half of the tide. Parking is $5.00, and there is a $5.00 launch fee for kayakers. The boatyard is open for day use only. Head toward Sebasco on Ridge Road and turn right onto Gomez Road where there is a sign for Brewer's Boat Yard. Follow this a short distance down to the boatyard. Check in at the office for parking directions. The Bethel Point Boat Yard is used for launching from the public boat ramp at Hen Cove. Parking at the ramp is by permit only for town residents, but you may launch from the ramp after parking at the adjacent Bethel Point Boat Yard. From Route 24 turn left onto Cundys Harbor Road after crossing the Gurnet Strait bridge. Follow this road for 3.2 miles and turn right onto Bethel Point Road before you come to the town of Cundys Harbor. Follow this road to its end at the boat ramp and turn into the boatyard on your right. There is a fee of $5.00 to park your car at the boatyard. If no one is around, go up the steps to the house on the hill; you should find a box to deposit your fee. There is a portable toilet available in the boatyard. You will need to paddle around the exposed Cundys Point to reach the river mouth from this launch site.

LOCAL ATTRACTIONS: The towns along this stretch of the river are small and offer only a few lodging options and mostly take-out food service. However, the impressive Sebasco Harbor Resort (800–225–3819) and nearby Rock Gardens Inn (207–389–1339) offer full lodging and meal options. Both Bath and Brunswick, located to the north along Route 1, also offer numerous possibilities. The Peary-MacMillan Arctic Museum (207–725–3416) at Bowdoin College in Brunswick makes an interesting visit, with its memorabilia from these two Bowdoin alumni as well as North Greenland kayak artifacts and models.

Route 8

Barters Island and the Lower Sheepscot River

The Sheepscot River and its backwaters are picturesque and offer hours of exploring, though there are few public access points for a leg stretch or pit stop. You'll need to avoid the strong tidal runs both into and out of Knubble Bay on the western side of the river, but the river current itself is manageable for sea kayakers. Both the Cross River and the Back River on the eastern side are well protected and offer numerous quiet spots for leisurely paddling. You will want to be careful when paddling through the area marked Oven Mouth on the Cross River. While it isn't quite as intimidating as its name implies, it is a fast run of water and should be avoided during the middle of the tide. If you're able to time most of your exploring for a couple of hours on either side of high tide, you can follow the many fingers of the Cross River. If not, poke up into Parsons Creek until the timing is right for Oven Mouth.

There is a nice loop trip which launches and lands at Knickerbocker Island Park, which is just off the road entering Hodgdon Island. This is a Boothbay town park with some parking and a few picnic spots, but it can be crowded on summer weekends. The launch ramp puts you into protected waters at the Hodgdon Island bridge. From this point it is best to head north and explore the eastern side of Barters Island or make a quick jog to the west following the well-marked channel under the Barters Island bridge and out into the Sheepscot River. The current can be a little squirrelly under the bridge, but it is not difficult. The channels leading around the southern end of Barters are narrow for larger boats, so give them room to ease through these passages.

You have several options for exploring this area: You can do a simple circumnavigation of Barters if you are pressed for time (a little over 8 miles), you can circumnavigate and add a side trip on the Cross River, or you can head south to explore a beautiful group of islands clustered around Isle of Springs before heading along the western shore of Barters. There is usually fine seal-watching in this area, and this group of islands offers plenty of protected paddling—even down into Ebenecook Harbor. The combinations are many, and you can usually avoid working against the tide or any strong winds along the way.

If you'd like to include a decadent lunch stop, consider paddling south and across the Sheepscot River to Five Islands Lobster. You can land at the public ramp to the left of the big wharf, and after you're stuffed to the eyeballs with fresh lobsters and steamers (there's a grill and ice cream stand as well), you can explore the eastern shore of Macmahan Island and shoot back across the Sheepscot River. Don't be tempted to explore Goose Rock Passage unless you can time it perfectly with the slack tide. The currents in this passage and the Little Sheepscot can be unruly and unpredictable for sea kayakers.

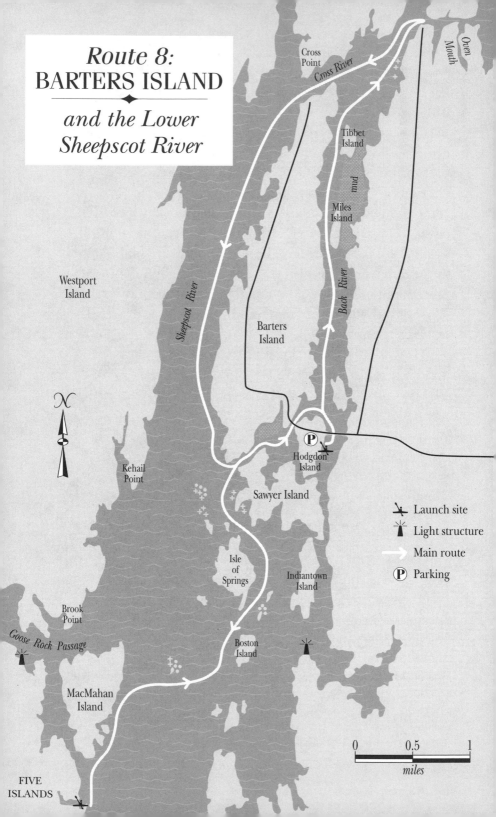

Route 8:
BARTERS ISLAND
◆
and the Lower Sheepscot River

Oven Mouth

Cross Point

Cross River

Tibbet Island

mud

Miles Island

Westport Island

Sheepscot River

Back River

Barters Island

P

Hodgdon Island

Kehail Point

Sawyer Island

Isle of Springs

Indiantown Island

Launch site

Light structure

Main route

P Parking

Brook Point

Goose Rock Passage

Boston Island

MacMahan Island

FIVE ISLANDS

0   0.5   1
miles

TRIP HIGHLIGHTS: Plenty of protected paddling and a quintessential Maine coastal lunch stop at Five Islands Lobster.

TRIP DURATION/LENGTH: As little or as much as you choose. A pleasant-paced paddle around Barters with side trips to explore islands to the south and even pass through Oven Mouth is still a reasonable 12 miles or so. You can add other options and mileage as you see fit.

NAVIGATIONAL AIDS: Chart 13293 Damariscotta, Sheepscot and Kennebec Rivers (1:40,000). Lighted gong buoy at entrance to Cross River; lighted buoy off Isle of Springs; can buoy marking entrance to Five Islands.

CAUTIONS: No public access except the launch site. Do not challenge unpredictable currents in Goose Rock Passage or Knubble Bay. The Oven Mouth at mid-tide is best avoided.

LAUNCH SITE: Knickerbocker Island Park is the only choice on this side of the Sheepscot between Boothbay and Wiscasset. From Route 1 follow signs to Boothbay Harbor for 9.6 miles. You'll see the Boothbay war statue just outside Boothbay Center (not Boothbay Harbor); follow the signs onto Barters Island Road to Hodgdon and Barters Island. It is approximately 1.5 miles to the turn into the parking area for Knickerbocker Island Park and Boat Ramp on the left just after the Hodgdon Island bridge.

LOCAL ATTRACTIONS: Five Islands Lobster (on the west side of the Sheepscot) sits at the very end of Route 127, which meanders from its turnoff north of the Bath bridge and across Georgetown Island. Nearby, Grey Havens Inn (800–431–2316) and Coveside Bed and Breakfast (800–232–5490) provide excellent lodging options. On the east side of the river, the town of Boothbay Harbor offers a wide variety of restaurants, lodging, and shops. Or, there's the Hodgdon Island Inn (207–633–7474) just a few minutes from the launch site and a short drive from Boothbay Harbor.

Barters Island and the Lower Sheepscot River

Route 9

![arrow]

Sheepscot River from Wiscasset Downstream

T he village of Wiscasset sits at the juncture of the Sheepscot and Back Rivers (this is not the same as the Back River found on the east side of the Sheepscot). This can create some large eddies and confusing areas on a flooding tide as water moves up the Sheepscot and then bends to begin flowing in the opposite direction down the Back River to Montsweag Bay. The tide and even the direction of the tidal current can be difficult to predict along the Back River, and constricted areas like Cowseagan Narrows run too swiftly for kayakers. Because of these conditions and the lack of public access on the Back River and Montsweag Bay, this section is not easily paddled except by local outfitters with private access to a piece of shoreline and a healthy dollop of local knowledge. However, Wiscasset makes a nice launch site for exploring along the Sheepscot in both directions from this coastal village.

Wiscasset lays claim to being "the prettiest village in Maine," with its beautiful old homes and shady lanes that straddle Route 1. It does make a pleasant view from the water as long as you ignore the power station just south of town on the edge of the Back River. Launching in Wiscasset allows you to paddle either north up the Sheepscot River or paddle down the river to explore for a few hours or an entire day.

Heading south down the Sheepscot on a flooding tide, you should be careful to ferry across to a point just below the Route 1 bridge on the western shore of Davis Island and then hug that shoreline. If the flooding tide is at its strongest,

you will need to paddle hard across an eddy line just off the southern end of Davis Island. Keep your angle high and push hard for a few strokes, and you will cross this line and be able to paddle up into the large back eddy that forms to the east of Davis. You can see a triangle of turbulence that is created by a flooding tide at the junction of the two rivers. If you do not feel comfortable with the idea of paddling through this eddy line, simply wait until the current slackens before paddling south. Once you are beyond Davis Island, the remainder of the trip is quite placid.

    The Sheepscot River is a pastoral setting with homes

dotting the shoreline on both sides, and some nice contour to the riverbanks south of Hilton Point. You can paddle as far down the river as you feel comfortable, keeping an eye out for ospreys, blue herons, and a wide variety of shorebirds. The wooded areas along the river are active with passerine species during the spring and early summer. An occasional harbor seal will venture upriver, though these animals are far more numerous farther south on the ledges around Ram Island by Isle of Springs.

Unfortunately, there are no public-access areas along this stretch of the Sheepscot River until you get to Knickerbocker Island Park by the Hodgdon Island bridge (see Route 8). There are a few sites to ground out for a rest or picnic on the decks of rafted kayaks, but that's about it. Still, this makes a nice afternoon or morning paddle worked around exploring the village of Wiscasset and its many shops and restaurants.

TRIP HIGHLIGHTS: Seeing Wiscasset from the water and feeling superior to the poor souls that are backed up in this well known traffic bottleneck.

TRIP DURATION/LENGTH: As far as you're comfortable paddling round trip without a break from being in your boat.

NAVIGATIONAL AIDS: Chart 13293 Damariscotta, Sheepscot and Kennebec Rivers (1:40,000). Nun buoy off Davis Island; can buoy off Clough Point; lighted gong buoy at entrance to Cross River.

CAUTIONS: Currents off Davis Island and the entire Back River area on the west side of the Sheepscot River.

LAUNCH SITE: You can use the Wiscasset public boat ramp or the launch area in the small pool behind the railroad trestle at Pottle Cove. If you choose the latter, you'll have to have better timing; at high tide only the best of limbo moves will get you under the bridge, and when coming and going you'll need to contend with the flow under the bridge, which can be significant from either direction during the middle of the tide.

The public boat ramp has parking but can be very crowded

Sheepscot River from Wiscasset Downstream

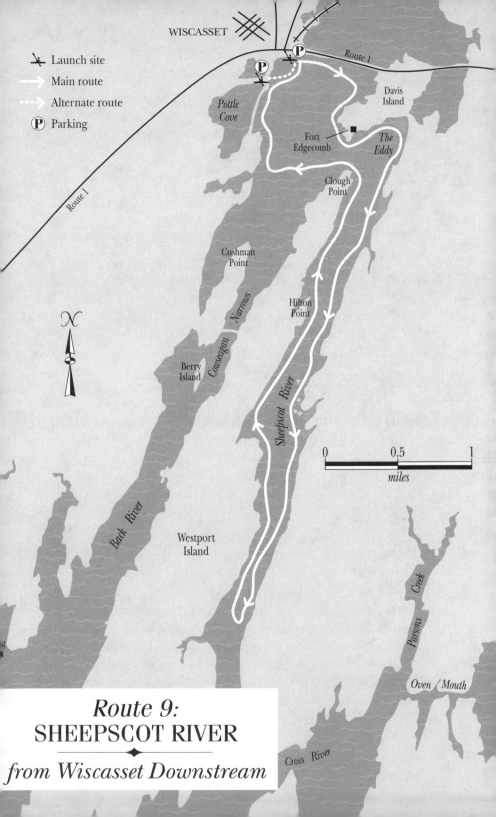

WISCASSET

Launch site
Main route
Alternate route
Ⓟ Parking

Route 1

Route 1

Pottle Cove

Davis Island

Fort Edgecomb

The Eddy

Clough Point

Cushman Point

Hilton Point

Narrows

Crousagan

Berry Island

Sheepscot River

N

0   0.5   1
miles

Westport Island

Back River

Creek

Parsons

Oven Mouth

Cross River

Route 9:
SHEEPSCOT RIVER
from Wiscasset Downstream

during peak use. Turn at Water Street just south of the Route 1 bridge and head to the area marked with PUBLIC PARKING and PUBLIC BOAT RAMP signs. For the smaller launch site behind the railroad tracks, turn left at the post office onto Fort Hill Road. Continue down the hill and to the right to a dirt parking area just before the tracks. Be careful not to park below any tide line (it's happened!).

LOCAL ATTRACTIONS: The entire village of Wiscasset is an attraction; its fine homes date from the late 1700s. You can pack lunch from the supplies at Treats or Sara's, both on Main Street (Route 1), or grab an ice cream cone or basket of fried food at Red's Eats. Wiscasset is renowned for its many varied antiques dealers, with enough choices to exhaust even the most die-hard shoppers. A scenic railroad runs along the river during the summer months.

Route 10

Sheepscot River from Wiscasset Upstream

Paddling up the Sheepscot River avoids any squirrely currents around Davis Island and explores this pleasant stretch of river to the north of Wiscasset at the backwaters of the Marsh River. As you leave the picturesque village of Wiscasset, stay fairly close to the shoreline while you're underneath the Route 1 bridge—the current is stronger in the middle of the river than along its shores. Once you are beyond the bridge you'll see two railroad rights-of-way over the river, one to your left at Clark Point and another farther upriver that you'll pass under. To the east is Cod Cove, a popular clamming site in the mudflats close to Route 1. Once you pass under the railroad trestle, you'll immediately feel the quiet settle in as you leave the noise and visual impact of Route 1 behind. There is plenty of exploring along this section of river that can extend into the backwaters of the Marsh River.

There are bald eagles along this section of the Sheepscot as well as blue herons, ospreys, and a variety of ducks and hawks. On our first trip in this area, we watched a bald eagle hit the water and rise with a fish in its talons, a crow pestering its every move. There are few homes along the shore, and the banks are often heavily wooded. We have spotted red foxes along the shore and sat quietly listening to squirrel spats and a cacophony of bird calls.

Less than 4 miles up the river from the Route 1 bridge, the river takes a hard right and narrows suddenly. This is the

Sheepscot reversing falls, and during flood tide it can run very swiftly through a short drop with a few standing waves. A sea kayak is not responsive enough to take full advantage of these river play conditions, though you'll likely see white-water boaters having their fun. You should remain above the falls unless it is near slack. Paddling back out of the area below the drop is simply impossible except as the flood tide approaches slack. Other than this spot, you don't need to be overly concerned with tidal currents along this stretch of the Sheepscot River. They are typically gentle and will have less effect on sea kayakers than will the wind direction.

TRIP HIGHLIGHTS: Quiet exploring along a beautiful stretch of river, bald eagles, great blue herons and numerous species of ducks.

TRIP DURATION/LENGTH: The round trip from Wiscasset to the reversing falls is 8 or more miles, depending on your side trips into backwaters of the Marsh River.

NAVIGATIONAL AIDS: Chart 13293 Damariscotta, Sheepscot and Kennebec Rivers (1:40,000).

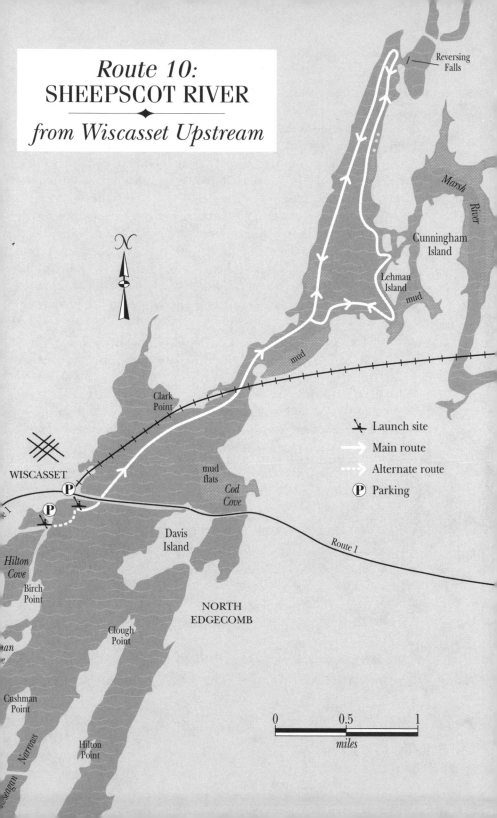

Route 10:
SHEEPSCOT RIVER
◆
from Wiscasset Upstream

Reversing
Falls

Marsh
River

Cunningham
Island

Lehman
Island

mud

mud

Clark
Point

Launch site

Main route

Alternate route

P Parking

WISCASSET

P

mud
flats

Cod
Cove

P

Davis
Island

Route 1

Hilton
Cove

Birch
Point

NORTH
EDGECOMB

Clough
Point

Cushman
Point

Narrows

Hilton
Point

0   0.5   1
miles

CAUTIONS: Sheepscot reversing falls about 4 miles upriver and the entire Back River on the west side of the Sheepscot River.

LAUNCH SITE: You can use the Wiscasset public boat ramp or the launch area in the small pool behind the railroad trestle at Pottle Cove. If you choose the latter, you'll have to have better timing; at high tide only the best of limbo moves will get you under the bridge, and when coming and going you'll need to contend with the flow under the bridge, which can be significant from either direction during the middle of the tide.

    The public boat ramp has parking but can be very crowded during peak use. Turn at Water Street just south of the Route 1 bridge and head to the area marked with PUBLIC PARKING and PUBLIC BOAT RAMP signs. For the smaller launch site behind the railroad tracks, turn left at the post office onto Fort Hill Road. Continue down the hill and to the right to a dirt parking area just before the tracks. Be careful not to park below any tide line (it's happened!).

LOCAL ATTRACTIONS: The entire village of Wiscasset is an attraction; its fine homes date from the late 1700s. You can pack lunch from the supplies at Treats or Sara's, both on Main Street (Route 1), or grab an ice cream cone or basket of fried food at Red's Eats. Wiscasset is renowned for its many varied antiques dealers, with enough choices to exhaust even the most die-hard shoppers. A scenic railroad runs during the summer months.

Damariscotta
to Pemaquid

Route 11

Damariscotta River

Part of a rich and varied ecosystem, the Damariscotta River is a wonderful place to explore by sea kayak. On one trip we observed a pair of bald eagles, a nesting pair of ospreys, several species of gulls, harbor seals, and blue herons, along with huge flotillas of jellyfish and horseshoe crabs. And that was after a mere hour of paddling away from the town landing! The river also supports a thriving aquaculture economy renowned for its oysters.

The river reaches as far inland as Damariscotta Mills, where fish ladders aid the alewife run in the spring and lure a host of birds intent on feeding off of this seasonal run and the rich mudflats of Salt Bay. The tidal flow in and out of Salt Bay can create significant turbulence and even two reversing falls, which serve as play spots for white-water kayakers and canoeists. Most of Salt Bay is exposed mudflats at low tide. It is best to begin your trip at the Damariscotta town landing, which is below any of the turbulence at the bridge between the towns of Newcastle and Damariscotta. While the river is narrowed at low tide, it maintains a fairly deep channel that allows passage to most small fishing vessels and yachts. There is lots to explore along the banks on either side, though the western side of the river is less developed.

The 3.5 mile paddle down to Dodge Point makes a great day trip, with plenty of leisure for exploring by kayak or on foot at the Dodge Point Preserve. This 506-acre preserve, administered by the Bureau of Parks and Lands with assistance from the Damariscotta River Association,

features trails that meander along the shoreline and through the forests along the river. These trails can be accessed by boaters landing at the preserve or from the trailhead off River Road (trailhead parking on River Road is too far from the shoreline for use as a launch site). The area is rarely crowded and makes a great picnic spot during your river explorations. Besides landing at the dock, which is marked with a small DAMARISCOTTA RIVER ASSOCIATION sign, you may land at any of the beaches to the north. At high tide these may be mere pockets of gravel, but there are fine ledges for a stretch on warm rock. Please help prevent bank erosion by not scrambling up any dirt banks to access trails. Instead, walk the shoreline ledges to reach the trail at the seasonal dock. You'll find a shady picnic area here as well.

Continue downriver as far as you feel comfortable, knowing that you'll have to backtrack to return home. You'll want to be aware of the tide and the wind direction. A strong southwesterly wind can channel up the river and make your paddle out somewhat strenuous—but it'll let you fly back to the town landing. Even when you're opposing the wind, there are points of land you can hide behind for a breather, though it's more difficult to find protection at low tide. The tide is reasonably gentle except where constricted. Just below Dodge Point, Glidden Ledge off Fitch Point can create a minor tide rip at half tide or higher. At lower tides you'll find it rocky going; large eddies are manageable but can be disconcerting to novices. If you'd like to camp overnight, continue downriver for about 10 miles to Fort Island, a thirty-seven-acre island managed by the Bureau of Parks and Lands. There are extremely powerful currents around this island. It is best to approach at slack tide or hug the eastern shore of the river and wait until things calm before ferrying across for a landing. Fort Island has a large camping area on its southeast corner; a privy sits just beyond the stone wall west of the campsite. The camping area can be crowded during the summer season. Hodgsons Island, which sits just to the east of Fort, is under the care of the Damariscotta River Association and is open for day use.

TRIP HIGHLIGHTS: Exploring Dodge Point Preserve. Observing bald eagles, harbor seals, horseshoe crabs, jellyfish, and ospreys.

TRIP DURATION/LENGTH: The round-trip paddle to Dodge Point from the Damariscotta town landing is only 7 miles but offers plenty of meandering by kayak or on foot to make this a full day of exploring. We've even zipped out and back for a quick afternoon jaunt to unwind during the early-spring months, catching some bird-watching along the way. If you have a full day, you can't beat Dodge Point as a picnic site and rest stop. This makes a fine family trip, since there are never long stretches in the boat, and you'll find plenty of places to burn off energy on land.

NAVIGATIONAL AIDS: Chart 13293 Damariscotta, Sheepscot and Kennebec Rivers (1:40,000). Glidden Ledge day beacon.

CAUTIONS: Rips at Glidden Ledge off Fitch Point. Extremely powerful currents around Fort Island.

LAUNCH SITE: The Damariscotta town landing is an all-tide facility with parking, but you may have trouble snagging an eight hour parking slot during the summer unless you get there early. As with

Damariscotta River

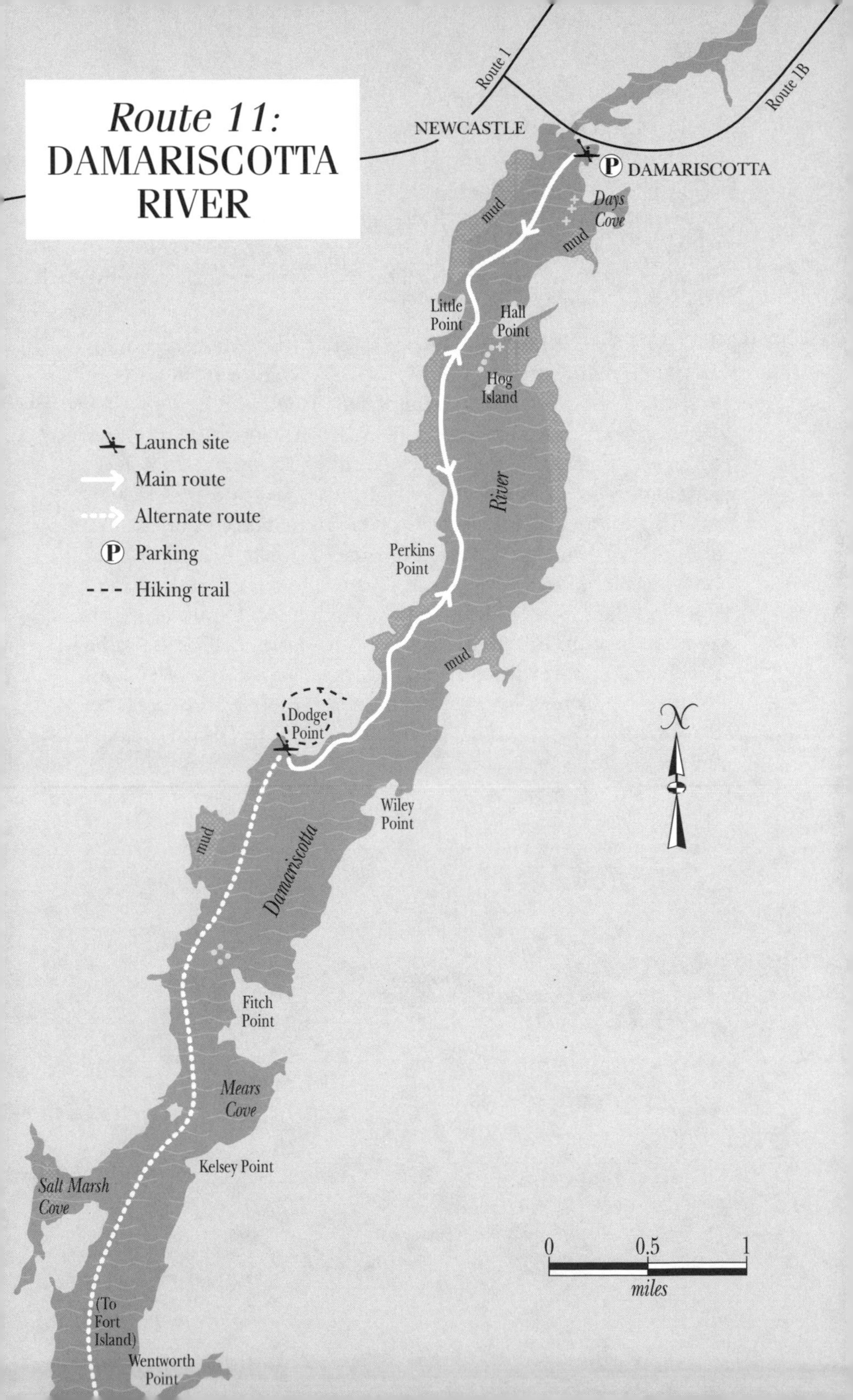

Route 11:
DAMARISCOTTA RIVER

Route 1

Route 1B

NEWCASTLE

℗ DAMARISCOTTA

mud

Days Cove

mud

Little Point

Hall Point

Hog Island

River

↙ Launch site

→ Main route

⇢ Alternate route

℗ Parking

--- Hiking trail

Perkins Point

mud

Dodge Point

Wiley Point

mud

Damariscotta

N

Fitch Point

Mears Cove

Kelsey Point

Salt Marsh Cove

(To Fort Island)

Wentworth Point

0   0.5   1
miles

most coastal towns, parking is at a premium during the summer months. You may need to drop off your boats, find parking outside the downtown area, and walk back to the ramp.

The town of Damariscotta is just off Route 1; the turnoff is clearly marked from both directions. The boat ramp is marked with a blue sign just off Main Street to the west of the Mobil station. You can see the ramp if you are crossing the bridge from the Newcastle side.

LOCAL ATTRACTIONS: There are a host of interesting shops along the main stretch of road through downtown Damariscotta. For picnic supplies, head to the Rising Tide Food Co-op or Shop 'N Save, both of which are on the Route 1B spur north of town, or to the small grocery at the town landing. There are numerous lodging choices in the area, especially along Route 129/130 heading towards Bristol, where bed-and-breakfast establishments abound. Within easy walking distance of the launch ramp, you'll find the Breakfast Place (a fine start to the day) and the King Eider Pub and Backstreet Landing, both serving local seafood and brew. You can pick up trail maps at the Dodge Point Preserve trailhead, which sits off River Road several miles beyond Newcastle. The Round Top Center for the Arts has exhibitions and programs throughout the year. It can be found on Route 1B just outside town.

Route 12

Johns Bay

Johns Bay offers a wide range of sea kayaking experiences and skill requirements. The bay's upper reaches and the Johns River offer a protected and pleasant afternoon's paddle exploring a shoreline of salt-water farms with a picturesque backdrop of evergreens and granite ledges. But Johns Bay has its wilder side. It opens to the south, and a long fetch will often send a sizable swell into the lower bay, the same swell that is crashing on Pemaquid Point just a short hop to the east. If this swell is opposed by a strong offshore breeze, things can get very choppy and confused. These are not conditions for a relaxing paddle.

As the swell rolls into Johns Bay, it can create some spectacular spray and rebound on the ledges outside the Thread of Life. However, there is plenty of deep water in the Thread of Life, so you can often paddle this passage safely while waves are crashing on nearby ledges. If your bracing skills and balance aren't up to the challenge, duck behind Hay Island to the north and enjoy the views across the ledges and out to Thrumcap Island.

Circumnavigation of Rutherford Island

A circumnavigation of Rutherford Island makes a fine day's paddle as long as you aren't bucking any strong winds, especially from the south. The perfect scenario has you launching in South Bristol at or close to slack tide, then paddling with the ebb tide down the Damariscotta River and the western shore of Rutherford. As the afternoon sea breezes begin to build, you'll have them at your back as you

begin the Johns Bay portion of the loop and work your way
up the eastern shore of Rutherford. Obviously, such turns of
luck are rare, but this trip rewards good planning and a wise
consideration of tide and wind.

The Gut in South Bristol can be problematic, because
predicting the direction of its flow isn't as simple as
checking a tide table. The Gut runs east–west and connects
the Damariscotta River and Johns Bay, so that wind and
water conditions on either side of it determine the direction
of its current. This flow can exceed 3 knots; waiting for its
lighter moments is well advised. At high tide there's only
about 3 feet of clearance under the bridge. If it's a spring
tide or you're feeling claustrophobic, you can wait for the
bridge to open for a larger boat and then tag along. Chat
up the bridge keeper on a slow day and the bridge may
even swing open just for you (larger boats signal with three
toots). There is little maneuvering room for the bigger
boats, so stay well to the side and let them pass.

You can stop at Christmas Cove on the western shore
for lunch and a leg stretch at Coveside Marine, where there
is a boat ramp. Christmas Cove is a favorite stopover for
many large yachts and offers a nice respite from the wind if

Johns Bay

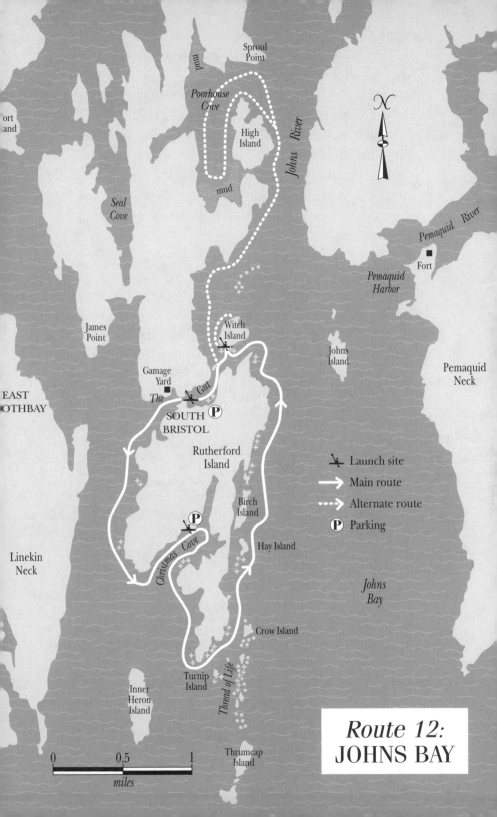

Sproul
Point

pond

*Poorhouse
Cove*

High
Island

mud

Johns River

mud

*Seal
Cove*

ort
and

Pemaquid River

Fort

*Pemaquid
Harbor*

James
Point

Witch
Island

Johns
Island

**Pemaquid
Neck**

Gamage
Yard

*The
Gut*

**SOUTH
BRISTOL**

Ⓟ

**EAST
OTHBAY**

Rutherford
Island

Birch
Island

Ⓟ

Christmas Cove

Hay Island

**Linekin
Neck**

*Johns
Bay*

Crow Island

Turnip
Island

Thread of Life

Inner
Heron
Island

Thrumcap
Island

🛶 Launch site

→ Main route

┈➤ Alternate route

Ⓟ Parking

Route 12:
JOHNS BAY

0   0.5   1
miles

𝒩

needed. Witch Island, which sits just to the northeast of South Bristol's harbor, is owned by National Audubon Society and open to the public from sunrise to sunset. There are pit toilets and hiking paths around the island. A caretaker lives on the island during the warmer months. There are stairs from the small cove on the town side of the island, but during high tide it's tough to secure your boat. You'll find a pocket beach on the northern side, and from there you can access the blue trail that marks the island's perimeter.

Other Options

As an alternative route, you can explore the upper reaches of Johns Bay and the Johns River, which is pastoral and offers lots of protection. Or rather than circumnavigating Rutherford, simply explore either the western shore or eastern shore (depending on conditions) as an out-and-back trip. (See also Colonial Fort Pemaquid, Route 13.)

TRIP HIGHLIGHTS: Wildly ranging conditions and spectacular scenery. The picturesque working harbor of South Bristol.

TRIP DURATION/LENGTH: Circumnavigating Rutherford Island is a full day of about 12 miles, depending on how many nooks and crannies you explore along the way. Depending on the conditions, this 12-mile trip can be a trying paddle, so be conservative in your planning and ready to shift to a backup plan if needed.

NAVIGATIONAL AIDS: Chart 13293 Damariscotta, Sheepscot and Kennebec Rivers (1:40,000). Day beacons on west side of gut; Christmas Cove beacons; can buoy off Shipley Point.

CAUTIONS: Swell running from the south, strong winds, exposure around southern end of Rutherford Island. Quick current through The Gut in South Bristol.

LAUNCH SITE: Use the Bittersweet Landing Boat Yard in South Bristol (207–644–8731). The town dock is usually crowded and parking is nearly impossible to find. Michael Nyboe at Bittersweet charges only $5.00 for kayak launching/landing and overnight parking (you'll need to leave your keys with him). The launch ramp at Bittersweet is all-tide and paved; it puts you right into the protection of the harbor on the east side of the gut. To reach it, take Route 129 out of Damariscotta and into South Bristol. Just 0.4 mile after you cross the South Bristol bridge, take a left onto Landing Lane and look for the BITTERSWEET sign on your left.

LOCAL ATTRACTIONS: You can purchase lobsters, sandwiches, and other goodies in South Bristol for the day or relax on the deck of Farrin's with some steamers and a lobster dinner after a hard day's paddling. Just west of The Gut is the Gamage Boatyard, which produced numerous fishing schooners for the Gloucester and New Bedford fleets as well as the *Mary Day*, *Shenandoah*, and *Clearwater*, all traditional wooden vessels active today. Lodging is available in Christmas Cove at Coveside Inn (207–644–8282) as well as numerous lodging establishments along the stretch between South Bristol and Damariscotta.

Johns Bay

Tidal Cycles in Maine

Tourists have been known to ask, "Where did all the water go?" when they look across an expanse of mudflat that was brimming full earlier in the day. As a sea kayaker, you should have a pretty good idea of where all the water went and when it might be coming back. The tidal cycle in Maine is semidiurnal, meaning we have two high and two low tides each day (actually over the course of each twenty-four hours and fifty minutes). This means that the time between high and low tide is about six hours.

The exact times of these high (flood) and low (ebb) tides shift slightly each day. If high tide is 9:00 A.M. on one day in a particular location, it will occur at about 9:25 P.M. that evening and again at 9:50 the following morning. As you move east from Portland to Bar Harbor, the time of a given tide will be earlier (in this case by around twenty-one minutes).

Maine has a significant tidal range (difference between high and low water). It varies from about 8 feet around Portland to nearly 28 feet in Eastport, so the tides here can cover and uncover a lot of real estate over the course of their cycle. The flow of water created by the rise and fall of the tide (tidal current) can be significant, especially where it's constricted. As you paddle and explore Maine's coast, you'll need to be aware of the tides and their timing. Almost any marine chandlery or paddle-sport shop will sell tide tables, which list the high and low tides each day for reference locations such as Portland or Bar Harbor. From these locations you can use a correction factor and find the tide for your paddling location (or reasonably close to it).

Route 13

Colonial Fort Pemaquid

Colonial Fort Pemaquid, a state park and museum, overlooks Pemaquid Harbor and sits across Johns Bay from South Bristol. The fort (actually the site of several forts built over the years from 1630 to 1729) and museum are open to the public for a small fee, or you can roam the grounds on your own. This is a convenient launch site. Exploring the area makes a great trip for kids with lots of options for a full day or a few hours of exploring. You can include numerous stops for a picnic or a swim in your plans.

There is a sandy launch ramp at the base of the large parking lot attached to the restaurant and museum buildings. This puts you into the well-protected waters of the inner harbor and the mouth of the Pemaquid River. You'll enjoy leisurely paddling with little exposure to the wind as you explore the river's gentle and shallow waters. At low tide some areas will be exposed, blocking passage into Coombs Cove and the area where the river narrows to more streamlike dimensions as it passes under Route 130.

You can also head out into Pemaquid Harbor and the waters of Johns Bay. All the options of exploring the upper reaches of Johns Bay, the Johns River, and the eastern shore of Rutherford Island are open to you from this launch site (see Johns Bay, Route 12). You can make the moderate crossing to Witch Island across the bay for a picnic outing, or paddle just a short distance south along the Pemaquid shore to the town beach, a sandy crescent open to the public with showers, picnic tables, and a snack bar ($2.00 admission).

TRIP HIGHLIGHTS: Pleasant and protected exploring around Pemaquid Harbor. A trip to nearby Witch Island or the Pemaquid town beach.

TRIP DURATION/LENGTH: This trip can range from a couple of hours' entertainment for the kids to a full day of gunkholing the backwaters with a leisurely lunch stop.

NAVIGATIONAL AIDS: Chart 13293 Damariscotta, Sheepscot and Kennebec Rivers (1:40,000). Can buoy at Corvette Ledge.

CAUTIONS: Swell running from the south on crossing to Witch Island. Extremely hazardous conditions at Pemaquid Point.

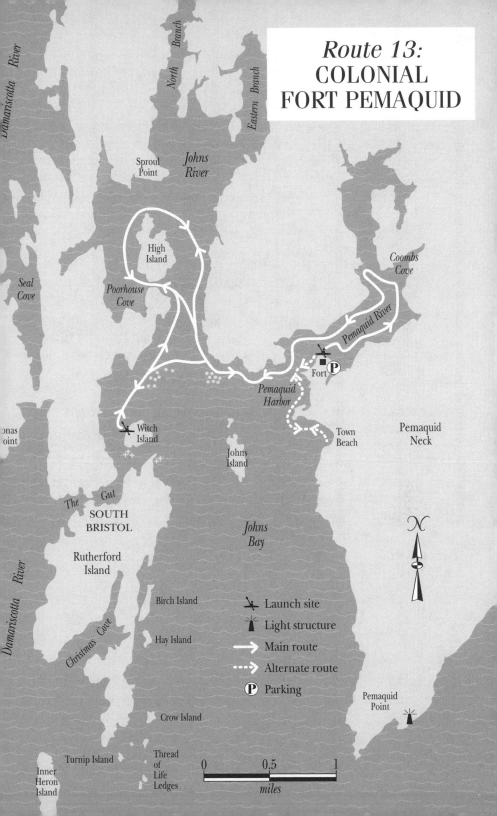

Route 13:
COLONIAL FORT PEMAQUID

Damariscotta River

North Branch

Eastern Branch

Sproul Point

Johns River

High Island

Poorhouse Cove

Seal Cove

Pemaquid River

Coombs Cove

Fort ⓟ

Pemaquid Harbor

onas oint

Witch Island

Johns Island

Town Beach

Pemaquid Neck

The Gut

SOUTH BRISTOL

Johns Bay

Rutherford Island

Damariscotta River

Birch Island

Christmas Cove

Hay Island

N

Crow Island

Pemaquid Point

Turnip Island

Inner Heron Island

Thread of Life Ledges

| ⚓ Launch site |
| ⚑ Light structure |
| → Main route |
| ⇢ Alternate route |
| ⓟ Parking |

0   0.5   1
miles

LAUNCH SITE: To reach Colonial Fort Pemaquid, take Route 130/129 out of Damariscotta and follow Route 130 through Bristol (*not* South Bristol). Continue on Route 130 towards New Harbor and look for the signs directing you to the fort. A dirt road leads past the fort to a large parking area adjacent to the restaurant and museum. The parking area is ample but can fill rapidly when the tour buses and weekend crowds descend on the area. You could also launch from the Pemaquid town beach ($2.00 fee), though it's a long carry to the water. Reach this site by turning onto Huddle Road off Route 130 and then continuing to the left (Colonial Fort Pemaquid is to the right) to a large PEMAQUID BEACH sign. There is a large parking lot.

LOCAL ATTRACTIONS: The Colonial Pemaquid Restaurant sits next to the launch ramp and offers a wide variety of fresh seafood, complete dinners, and even local brews. A short drive south on Route 130 puts you into the parking lot for the Pemaquid Point Light (fee). This lighthouse is one of the most scenic and best known on the Maine coast and offers a fine view across the waters from its rocky shoreline. There are several lodging options at Pemaquid Beach and north along Route 130 to Damariscotta.

WARNING: Do not be tempted to paddle along the shoreline of the Pemaquid Peninsula to access Pemaquid Point. This point is a dangerous area for kayakers. There is a long fetch, and the sizable swell usually runs through this area and spends its energy on Pemaquid's long, rocky shoreline. The rebound from these crashing waves can be treacherous—and there is no place to hide or land.

Colonial Fort Pemaquid

Round Pond
to Thomaston

Route 14

Rachel Carson Salt Pond Preserve

This out-and-back trip from Round Pond is a wonderful full-day paddle with a lunch stop at a very special place: the Rachel Carson Salt Pond Preserve. You can paddle right up to the quarter-acre tidal pool where Rachel Carson gathered much of the material for her book *The Edge of the Sea*. This site is managed by The Nature Conservancy and is open to the public year-round. It honors the work of Carson, who was also instrumental in starting the Maine chapter of The Nature Conservancy. The preserve covers a total of seventy-eight acres, most of it across Route 32 from the salt pond. You are welcome to hike the trails through woodlands and overgrown hay fields from the original Danforth farm, now the site of the Gosnold Arms Inn. The trailhead is directly across the road and marked by yellow blazes.

Along the shore you can see exposed bedrock that shows the folds and stripes of different colors as rocks melted and then recrystalized at different rates. This Bucksport Formation, created more than 420 million years ago, is even more noticeable at Pemaquid Point, a short drive away. (*Warning: Do not paddle there!*).

The small salt pond left behind as the tide recedes is a study of life in the intertidal zone. Three species of periwinkles occupy unique niches within the salt pond; dogwinkles, a larger relative of periwinkles, prey on barnacles, mussels, and smaller periwinkles. The pond is a beautiful conglomeration of colors: the streaked blue of mussel shells, the red and purple of Irish moss, and the

occasional bright green of dulse that washes into the area from deeper waters. As the tide recedes, you can sit in your boat and see starfish and sea urchins that remain submerged just outside the salt pond. At low tide, pull your kayak up on the rocky beach and explore the edges of the pond on foot. Please do not disturb or remove anything from the site or be tempted to toss any rocks into the pond.

The paddle from Round Pond is quite pleasant except in a strong southerly or southwesterly breeze. Louds Island, which is privately owned, has a beautiful shoreline. Beyond its southernmost point you can see small Bar Island and, beyond this, Ross and Haddock Islands. Just before you reach the Salt Pond Preserve, you'll pass Long Cove Point, a small finger of land protecting its deep-water cove. You won't see any signage for the preserve from the water, but there is a small wooden sign alongside the road and a set of wooden steps leading down to the salt pond less than 0.5 mile beyond Long Cove Point. The landing can be very slippery at low tide, and it is difficult to carry a kayak over this terrain. You'll need to be very careful and step between the seaweed-covered rocks. This landing is much easier on the upper half of a flood tide.

Beyond the salt pond is New Harbor, a working harbor that serves as a base for lots of lobster boats and trawlers. Back Cove—a finger of water running southwest from the mouth of New Harbor—is a nice place to explore, but stay well out of the way of any working boats that come and go

Rachel Carson Salt Pond Preserve

from their moorings there. If you look to the east from New Harbor, you can see Eastern Egg Rock about 6 miles out. A research project is trying to reestablish a puffin colony on this small island.

During the summer months you might want to consider a reasonably early start to avoid paddling into any prevailing southwest winds that may build from midmorning on. As the sea breeze builds in the afternoon, it is always nice to turn to the northeast for the return leg. This trip is designed to offer this combination of conditions, but you should still monitor the weather radio for any changes from the usual (if there is any "usual" when it comes to Maine weather!). A strong and sustained southerly or southwesterly may build challenging seas, and fog is always a possibility in these waters. If there are strong northerly or northwesterly winds, you should put off this trip for another day. You cannot chance losing ground against such a wind in this area, because there is little or no place to pull out once you are blown out of reach of the mainland's shore.

TRIP HIGHLIGHTS: Tidal pool explorations and paddling along a beautiful stretch of coastline.

TRIP DURATION/LENGTH: It is about 9 miles from Round Pond to the Rachel Carson Salt Pond Preserve and back. You may want to add a mile or two to this to explore New Harbor and Back Cove.

NAVIGATIONAL AIDS: Chart 13301 Muscongus Bay (1:40,000). Can buoy at Round Pond; lighted bell buoy off New Harbor.

CAUTIONS: Do not attempt in strong offshore winds. Tricky and possibly rough landing at tidal pool. Extremely hazardous conditions at Pemaquid Point.

LAUNCH SITE: Launch at the boat ramp in Round Pond just off Route 32. Look for the small blue sign. You'll find parking (day use only) and an easy launch for kayaks at all tides. The parking fee is $2.00. You can purchase cooked or live lobsters at the Fisherman's

Rachel Carson Salt Pond Preserve

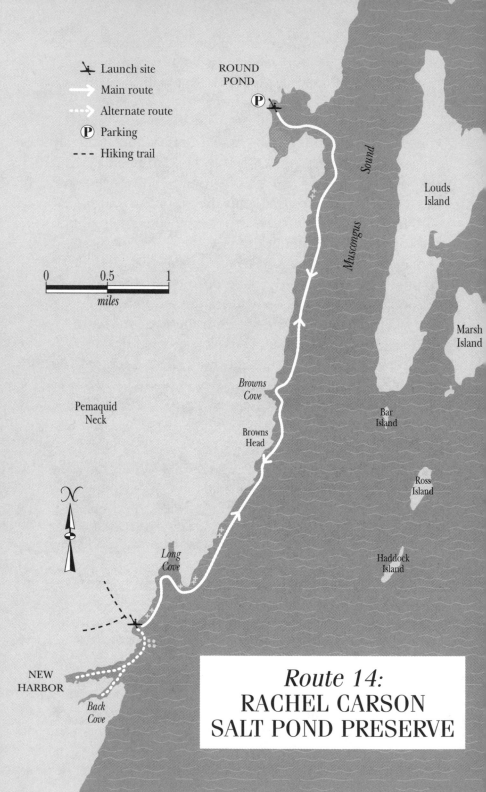

Route 14:
RACHEL CARSON
SALT POND PRESERVE

Launch site
Main route
Alternate route
P Parking
Hiking trail

ROUND
POND

P

Louds
Island

Muscongus

Sound

Marsh
Island

0   0.5   1
miles

Browns
Cove

Bar
Island

Browns
Head

Ross
Island

Pemaquid
Neck

N

Haddock
Island

Long
Cove

NEW
HARBOR

Back
Cove

Co-op adjacent to the parking area. If you are coming from north of Damariscotta, turn south onto Route 32 off Route 1 in Waldoboro. Follow Route 32 down the east side of the Pemaquid Peninsula to Round Pond. If you are coming from Route 1 south of Damariscotta, take Route 129/130 and then the Route 130 fork towards Bristol. In Bristol you can take Upper Bristol Mills Road directly into Round Pond, or take the scenic tour down to Pemaquid Point. From the point, follow Route 32 back up through New Harbor to Round Pond.

LOCAL ATTRACTIONS: Pemaquid Point (see Johns Bay, Route 12) is a must-see. The lighthouse is one of the most scenic anywhere, and the fisherman's museum is interesting. There is a fee for this visit. Almost every small town in this area offers lobsters, steamers, and mussels as well as picnic supplies. For more extensive facilities, Damariscotta and Waldoboro have large grocery stores and numerous restaurants. The best bread around is baked at Borealis Bread at the junction of Routes 1 and 220 just north of Waldoboro. For lodging, there's The Gosnold Arms Inn in New Harbor (207–677–3727) which adjoins part of the Rachel Carson Salt Pond Preserve, or the Briar Rose Bed and Breakfast in Round Pond (207–529–5478).

Route 15
▬ ▬ ▬ ▬ ▬ ▬ ▬ ▬ ▬ ▬ ▬ ▬ ▬ ▬ ▬ ▬ ➤

Round Pond to Hockomock Point

This trip takes you from Round Pond north to explore along Muscongus Harbor and Greenland Cove, with an educational lunch stop at Hockomock Point. The National Audubon Ecology Camp has a visitors center and nature trail here, both open to the public. The site has a small gravel boat ramp just below the boathouse on the point directly across from its Hog Island camp. (This ramp can be used for landing and a visit, but not as a launch site with parking.) Please do not land on Hog Island, but enjoy paddling its shoreline.

We recommend circumnavigating Hog Island because its largely undisturbed shoreline can offer some great bird-watching. If there's enough water, be sure to explore the narrow slit of water on the northern end of the island. In the spring you can sit and listen to an incredible array of birdcalls; the mudflats are a rich source of food for shorebirds in the area. Nesting blue herons, ospreys, and numerous songbird species find protection on this island. A pair of bald eagles has been attempting to nest on the Crotch Islands just off the eastern shore. Please do not disturb any birds that are on their nests or feeding along the shoreline.

Just off the northeast end of Hog Island is Crow Island, which is open to the public. Tent sites may be staked out by overnight campers, but the ledges on the south end offer fantastic views and a nice stretch in the sun (beware of poison ivy just off the ledges). To the northeast of Crow is Strawberry Island, another small island open to the public.

Strawberry Island is not marked on the chart but sits directly across the channel from Oar Island. There's a nice set of ledges on the northwest end for sunning and a picnic.

Hockomock Channel and the waters around Bremen Long Island are wonderful places to explore. If you don't mind a little mileage, consider paddling up Hockomock Channel and around the north end of Bremen Long Island. If you're paddling against the tide up Hockomock Channel, use the back eddies on either side of the channel; various points of land will help you. The same goes for Flying Passage on the east side of Bremen Long Island, which has a moderate current. You can make headway against the current in this area, but you'll find easier going along the shoreline.

Hungry Island, to the east, is a protected island (not open to the public) that deserves a circumnavigation if you don't mind adding to your paddling mileage once again. Then you can continue down the eastern shore of Bremen Long Island and around its southern point in the well-marked channel. Head towards the eastern shoreline of Hog Island to continue that circumnavigation before rounding its southern point for the return to Round Pond.

This entire trip offers fair protection from a variety of wind directions. If there has been a strong and sustained south or southwesterly wind, seas that are running up Muscongus Sound between Round Pond and Hog Island can make your return leg across this channel a bumpy ride. The crossing is still only a bit more than 0.5 mile and you can hug the western shore of Louds Island before setting an advantageous ferry angle across to Round Pond if needed.

You're bound to see other kayakers in this area, since the islands of Crow, Thief, Havener Ledge, Strawberry, and Little Marsh are all made available for overnight camping by the Bureau of Parks and Lands.

TRIP HIGHLIGHTS: Excellent bird-watching, island explorations, and a visit to the National Audubon Ecology Camp.

TRIP DURATION/LENGTH: You should plan on a full day of paddling, but there are plenty of places to take out and stretch or have a snack along the way. If you want to keep your mileage low, use a stop at Hockomock Point as the turnaround for a pleasant paddle of just over 6 miles. You can include a nature trail hike at the National Audubon Center for a full day of exploring. If you're up for more kayaking mileage, a trip around Bremen Long Island adds another 6 miles, and it's easy to paddle still more as you explore this beautiful area. The complete trip up Hockomock Channel and around both Hungry and Bremen Long Islands with a circumnavigation of Hog Island works out to a bit less than 14 miles.

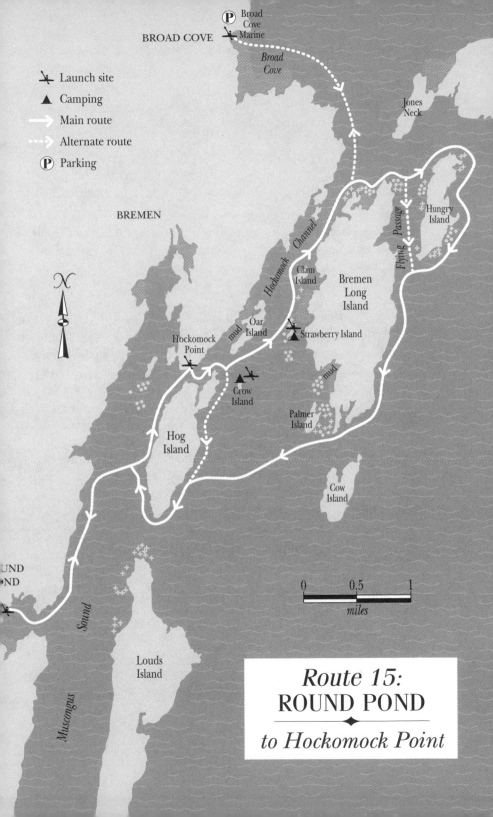

P Broad
Cove
Marine

*Broad
Cove*

Jones
Neck

Launch site

Camping

Main route

Alternate route

P Parking

BREMEN

Hungry
Island

N

Flying Passage

Hockomock Channel

Clam
Island

Bremen
Long
Island

mud

Oar
Island

Hockomock
Point

Strawberry Island

Crow
Island

mud

Palmer
Island

Hog
Island

Cow
Island

UND
ND

0   0.5   1
miles

Sound

Louds
Island

Route 15:
ROUND POND
◆
to Hockomock Point

Muscongus

NAVIGATIONAL AIDS: Chart 13301 Muscongus Bay (1:40,000). Can at Round Pond; cans in Lower Narrows; nun buoys off Oar Island; day beacon at Flying Passage.

CAUTIONS: Very choppy conditions if the tide is opposed by a strong, sustained wind. Mid-tide current through Flying Passage and Hockomock Channel can be swift.

LAUNCH SITE: Round Pond is a good site for paddling these waters. There are other public launch sites above Keene Neck at Medomak and at Dutch Neck, but there have been several car break-ins over the past few years. Neither site is a good choice for overnight parking if you are planning to camp on any of the public islands in this area. Broad Cove Marine (207–529–5186) has an all-tide gravel boat ramp and secure parking for a fee of $7.00. Broad Cove is just north of Hockomock Channel.

To reach Round Pond from Route 1 south of Damariscotta, take Route 129/130 and then the Route 130 fork towards Bristol. In Bristol you can take Upper Bristol Mills road directly into Round Pond, or take the scenic tour down to Pemaquid Point. From the point, follow Route 32 back up through New Harbor to Round Pond.

Broad Cove Marine can be reached by heading south on Route 32 out of Waldoboro for 7 miles. Just past the Bremen Town Office and Fire Department, turn left onto Medomak Road and drive 1.8 miles to the end, staying left at the final fork. There is a gravel boat ramp and parking up the hill.

LOCAL ATTRACTIONS: This is a kayaker's paradise; you could easily spend a week or more exploring this area. Muscongus Bay is one of the richest lobstering grounds on the Maine coast. There is plenty of good local seafood to be found in any of the coastal villages that dot its shoreline. The Gosnold Arms Inn (207–677–3727) in New Harbor and the Briar Rose Bed and Breakfast (207–529–5478) in Round Pond offer lodging with easy access to the water. The town of Friendship, which lies directly east of Bremen Long Island, is a working harbor full of fishing vessels with a few small stores and take-out restaurants. There are several kayak-friendly lodging options in Friendship (see Friendship, Route 16, for more information on lodging).

Round Pond to Hockomock Point

Route 16

■ ■ ■ ■ ■ ■ ■ ■ ■ ■ ■ ■ ■ ➤

Friendship

Muscongus Bay has become a very popular sea kayaking area over the last ten years. The cluster of public islands on the western side of the bay is almost always full of campers during the summer months. The eastern side of Muscongus Bay is every bit as beautiful, but its only public-access point is a small paved ramp (with no parking) just to the east of Friendship Harbor. So you'll need to be comfortable staying in your boat or heading west to the shores of a public-access island. You may see kayak groups landing on some of the other islands in this area, but this is by permission of the private owner only and does not grant access to any other boaters.

The large islands in this area beg to be circumnavigated, and it's a real toss-up as to which ones you choose as your target. A nice loop trip takes you from Friendship Harbor around Friendship Long Island and Cranberry Island then up Otter Island Passage past the western shore of Morse Island. In typical summer conditions, in which southwesterly breezes build through the late morning and afternoon, you're best off heading west on the early legs of your trip to catch a tailwind or at least paddle out of the prevailing breezes during your return leg. Friendship Harbor is a traditional working Maine harbor that offers little in terms of food or groceries. It's a great place to view the workings of lobster boats as they pull in for the day; you might also spot the occasional Friendship Sloop, a vessel designed for working these waters and produced by the Wilbur Morse Boat Yard in Friendship at the close of the

nineteenth century. These boats became obsolete when
marine engines were developed, but they have thrived as
lovingly restored yachts.

Another nice paddling loop would take you around the
southern end of Gay Island and through the cluster of small
islands (Ram, Eagle, Stone, and Seavey) that sit between
Caldwell and McGee Islands. From there you can continue
on your loop back toward Gay Island. If you are on the
upper half of the tide, you can pass through the narrow
channel between the northern end of Gay Island and
Pleasant Point. This beautiful little stretch of water is well
protected and full of feeding shorebirds and wading birds.
You'll actually paddle over the compacted mud and gravel
bar between Gay Island and Pleasant Point that residents
use when vehicular access to Gay Island is needed. Maine
author Elisabeth Ogilvie lives on Gay Island, and many of
her books include descriptions of this area.

One way to build a rest and lunch stop into a paddle
around eastern Muscongus Bay is to extend a loop trip all
the way to Port Clyde. Here you may land at the public boat
ramp adjacent to the ferry terminal. You'll need to keep a
sharp eye out, for the boat traffic is constant, and there is

little patience with kayakers. Make sure to get your kayaks away from the ramp and out of the way if you pull in for lunch. At low tide you can also land on the small cobble beach to the northwest of Marshall Point Light. This landing disappears at higher tide levels and requires calm conditions. There is a portable toilet on the site, as well as some nice places to stretch out for a picnic lunch.

If you are faced with a windy day or crave placid conditions, you can paddle the waters to the north of Crotch Island, exploring the Back and Meduncook Rivers until they narrow to less than a kayak's width. During the summer months you'll find blue herons, turtles, kingfishers, and loads of horseshoe crabs in these waters. The shoreline is dotted with farmhouses and largely undeveloped.

TRIP HIGHLIGHTS: Watching lobster boats at their trade and Friendship Sloops in their natural habitat. Marshall Point Lighthouse and a wealth of islands to circumnavigate.

TRIP DURATION/LENGTH: Paddling in the protected waters to the north of Crotch Island can cover up to 6 miles. The loop around Friendship Long Island and Cranberry Island is about 8.5 miles; it can be shortened by cutting off the Cranberry Island portion or lengthened by exploring to the west of Friendship Harbor as well. The trip around Gay Island and the islands between Caldwell and McGee is a little more than 9 miles. Continuing to Port Clyde adds another 2 miles or so; Marshall Point Light sits another 0.5 mile to the south.

NAVIGATIONAL AIDS: Chart 13301 Muscongus Bay (1:40,000). Can buoy off northeast point of Morse Island; nun buoy off southwest side of Gay Island; buoys at Goose Rock Ledge and Channel Rock; Marshall Point Light; day beacons in Friendship Harbor.

CAUTIONS: Strong winds and exposure from the south. Challenging conditions off Marshall Point. Very limited public access.

LAUNCH SITE: You can launch from the town ramp which sits on the east side of the small point that bars to Garrison Island. You

will need to park elsewhere. The folks at Friendship Harbor House Bed and Breakfast will allow kayakers to park their vehicles at the B&B which is less than 100 yards up the road, for $5.00 per day. You must call ahead to make sure there is room for your vehicle (207–832–7447). This is really the only reasonable option unless you are dropped in by sky hook. The public boat ramps to the west make trips in this area a bit of a haul or worse. The Friendship House Bed and Breakfast is on Bradford Point Road (*not* Bradford Point, shown on the chart). From the north take Route 97 south off Route 1, and follow this for about 10 miles until the speed limit drops as you enter the town of Friendship. Look for Bradford Point Road on your left and take this 1.3 miles to Friendship House. From the south use Route 220 off Route 1. Follow this route into Friendship; 0.2 mile after it becomes Route 97, you will see Bradford Point Road on your right.

LOCAL ATTRACTIONS: Port Clyde has restaurants and lodging and serves as the ferry terminal for folks heading to Monhegan Island, about 10 miles out to sea (not a recommended paddle). Marshall Point Light, which marks the eastern end of Muscongus Bay and the channel leading into Port Clyde, is open to the public and maintained by the town of St. George. In Friendship, lodging options include Friendship Harbor House Bed and Breakfast (207–832–7447 or 207–236–8797) and Harbor Hill Bed and Breakfast (207–832–6646). There are only take-out restaurants in Friendship.

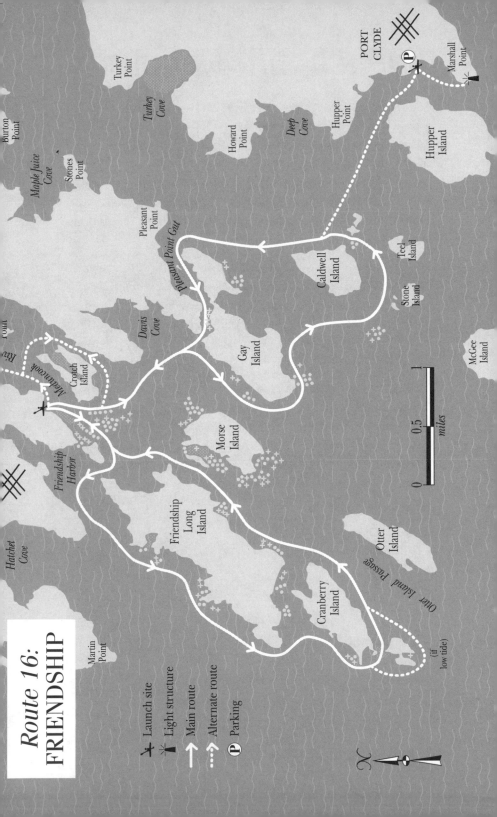

Route 16:
FRIENDSHIP

Launch site

Light structure

Main route

Alternate route

P Parking

miles

0   0.5   1

PORT CLYDE

P

Marshall Point

Hupper Point

Deep Cove

Howard Point

Turkey Point

Turkey Cove

Burton Point

Maple Juice Cove

Stones Point

Pleasant Point

Pleasant Point Gut

Davis Cove

Crotch Island

Medamook

River

Friendship Harbor

Hatchet Cove

Martin Point

Friendship Long Island

Morse Island

Gay Island

Caldwell Island

Teel Island

Stone Island

Hupper Island

McGee Island

Otter Island

Otter Island Passage

Cranberry Island

(if low tide)

Launch Site Etiquette

Some nonkayaking boaters have been known to grimace at the mere mention of sea kayaking. They roll their eyes and mutter less-than-flattering remarks about us as a group. Regrettably, some of these remarks are right on target. Often, one of the things that marks us at launch sites is our lack of organization and the length of time we tie up a ramp, oblivious to the boat trailers stacking up behind us like cars at the York, Maine tollbooth.

We've seen kayakers run back and forth to their car nine or ten times, grabbing last-minute items while they peel or don a layer of clothes. Their gear is piled up and toppling across the town float, while they rearrange the cooler items and fold the chart so it will fit in the chart case.

Try to organize your gear at home and use a mesh bag to carry it in. You don't really need to park on the ramp when you're loading or unloading kayaks from your vehicle. Consider packing and preparing your kayaks in an area that will not block access to the ramp. Then hand-carry or cart them to the water from your parking spot. Your courtesy will be appreciated, especially by folks who depend on the boat ramp for their livelihood.

Route 17

St. George River from Warren
to Thomaston

The St. George River winds its ways through the farmlands
and woods of the towns of Searsmont, Appleton, and
Union before becoming a tidal river in the town of
Warren. From Warren to Thomaston the river is an easy
half-day trip with the tide. You may choose to spot a vehicle
at either end for a one-way run, or paddle back to your put-
in with the return tide. The river is quiet and pastoral, with
tall grass and woodlands along the shore and an occasional
farmhouse. You'll cross under a total of five bridges, which
are the only noisy spots along the river. Ospreys, kingfishers,
and red-winged blackbirds are common sights. The woods
echo with birdcalls, from the lyrical song of the hermit
thrush to the raucous chatter of crows.

This is a relaxing paddle unless you're bucking a strong
southwesterly, which is not an uncommon scenario on a
summer afternoon. The tidal current is quite gentle but
picks up some strength after crossing under the Route 1
bridge and continues along the bend behind the Maine
State Prison. However, the current is always manageable,
though things can get choppy when opposed by the wind.
You can park your kayak in the mud along the shore for an
impromptu picnic or rest stop, and at either end of this trip
there are picnic and rest room facilities.

This makes a great float trip at a relaxing pace and a
nice alternative for a foggy-day paddle. It is also suitable for
canoes and recreational kayaks. You'll find a playground

and some short trails along the riverbank at the Warren put-in, and Thomaston offers plenty of interesting shopping and walking tours. It is easiest to run with the ebbing tide from Warren, since the put-in begins at a short riffle that makes for a difficult (although still manageable) takeout at this same spot. We've run it in both directions, however, and since the tide dictates the logistics, your plans will be made for you! You may even get lucky and have that afternoon southwesterly as a tailwind; you'll be running with the flooding tide for an easy ride into Warren.

TRIP HIGHLIGHTS: A tidal run through pastoral farmlands full of ospreys, great blue herons, and kingfishers.

TRIP DURATION/LENGTH: The one-way run is about 6.5 miles but with the help of the tidal current it can be paddled in only a couple of hours if needed. Slowing the pace is never a problem, since there are numerous slots of water through the grasses and a short paddle up the Oyster River outlet to explore. This is a full day of paddling if you're planning an out-and-back option, but either end offers a pleasant rest stop.

NAVIGATIONAL AIDS: USGS Topographical map: Thomaston (7.5 minute quadrangle).

CAUTIONS: Winds funneling along the river's course and swift mid-tide currents below the Route 1 bridge.

LAUNCH SITE: The Warren put-in is at Payson Park, which is just west of the intersection of Routes 90 and 131. The best place to launch is over the embankment below the footbridge. There is a short set of riffles where you may get a few scrapes, but this is shortlived. The Thomaston launch is reached by turning onto Knox Street at the traffic light in the center of town, marked by the Thomaston Cafe and Bakery (great picnic makings) on one corner and the Corner Gift Shop and Town Office on the other. If you are spotting a vehicle in Thomaston and then driving to the Warren put-in, head south on Route 1 from Thomaston for 1.0 mile, then turn right onto Route 131. Continue on Route 131 for 3.8 miles to the intersection with Route 90. Turn left onto Route 90, cross the river, and turn right into Payson Park.

St. George River from Warren to Thomaston

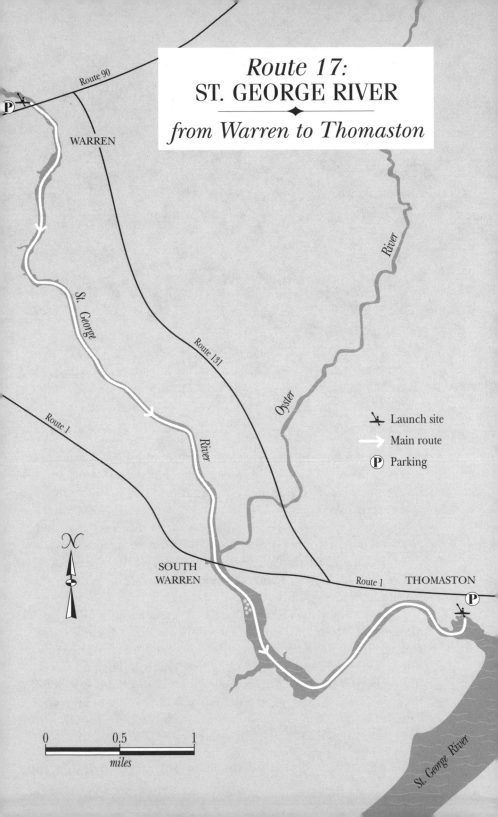

Route 17:
ST. GEORGE RIVER
from Warren to Thomaston

Route 90

WARREN

St. George

River

Route 131

Oyster

River

Route 1

Launch site

Main route

P Parking

N

SOUTH
WARREN

Route 1   THOMASTON

P

0   0.5   1

miles

St. George River

LOCAL ATTRACTIONS: Thomaston is full of historic homes and offers hours of walking and browsing along its shady streets and shopping areas. The Harbor View Restaurant is adjacent to the town ramp and serves lunch from 11:30 A.M. to 2:30 P.M., dinner from 5:00 to 9:00 P.M. The Thomaston Cafe and Bakery is a good place to stock up on picnic supplies. At Thomaston Books and Prints on Main Street, you can pick up a copy of Ben Ames Williams's *Come Spring*, which chronicles the life of the early settlers along the St. George River.

In Warren you can purchase picnic supplies at Frank's Market, just up the hill from Payson Park on Route 90. *Please note:* During the alewives run in late May, weirs are set across the river just below the second bridge in Warren. This will block travel on this section of the river during the run. You can double-check for their presence by looking downriver from the bridge in Warren center. Or try calling the town alewives number (207–273–2000) or the town office (207–273–2421).

St. George River from Warren to Thomaston

Route 18

St. George River from Thomaston to Port Clyde

U nless you're a brute of a paddler, you should take this trip as either a point-to-point paddle with vehicles spotted at either end, or as an out-and-back trip from Thomaston as far down the river as you feel like paddling and still have enough energy left to make the return leg a fun one. Paddling a tidal river is always fascinating, and this section of the St. George is particularly satisfying, both because of its gradual deepening and widening as you approach open water and because of the lack of obstructions along its course. There is only one place to pull out along the route, at Fort St. George, but there are places to duck into for protection from the wind if needed. The river is home to ospreys, great blue herons, kingfishers, cormorants, and several species of ducks. The tidal run carries alewives and other small bait fish and the stripers that feed on them. The stripers in turn bring fishermen working the river for the thrill of hooking into one of these big, boisterous fish.

The river is oriented along a southwest–northeast axis, so a wind from either of these directions is going to strengthen as it funnels down the river corridor. A southwest sea breeze will chop things up when opposing an ebbing tide. Still, the tidal current is never so strong that standing waves are created—like those on the Kennebec River, where the ebb tide can be extremely dangerous when opposed by a strong southwesterly. The out-and-back trip from Thomaston to Fort St. George works particularly well when

you get a free ride home with the prevailing breezes. We once paddled from Friendship to Thomaston in less than three hours, flying with the tide and the wind in our favor. You can play the river channel to maximize or minimize your exposure to the tidal current, and the land contours to protect or expose you to the wind direction.

There are several large and protected coves along the lower St. George: Maple Juice, Turkey, Watts, Otis, and Broad. None of these has any facilities, and most are quite muddy at low tide, but sometimes it's nice to be able to sit still, tucked into a notch of some cove, or to raft up for some refreshments away from the main channel. Fort St. George, where you can pull out for a welcome stretch and lunch stop, sits on the hills overlooking the river from the eastern bank on Fort Point just a bit over 3 miles below the town of Thomaston. There isn't much left of the fort except some earthworks. The site is managed by the Bureau of

Parks and Lands. At low tide this area is very muddy; you'll need to do some nimble stepping to avoid sinking to your ankles.

If you do choose to paddle the full length of the river between Thomaston and Port Clyde, make sure to plan carefully with both tide and wind direction in mind. If the winds are variable or less than 10 knots, you might consider letting the tidal current make your decisions. If a north-northeast or south-southwest wind is blowing at more than 10 knots, consider planning your trip to use the wind direction even if it means the tide isn't in your favor. Obviously, this trip rewards good planning, and if you can't work wind and tide factors in your favor, save it for another day. There's no reason to make this hard work. Part of good planning is knowing when to choose another route or another day for your trip!

TRIP HIGHLIGHTS: Approaching the sea along this historic river. Marshall Point Lighthouse in Port Clyde.

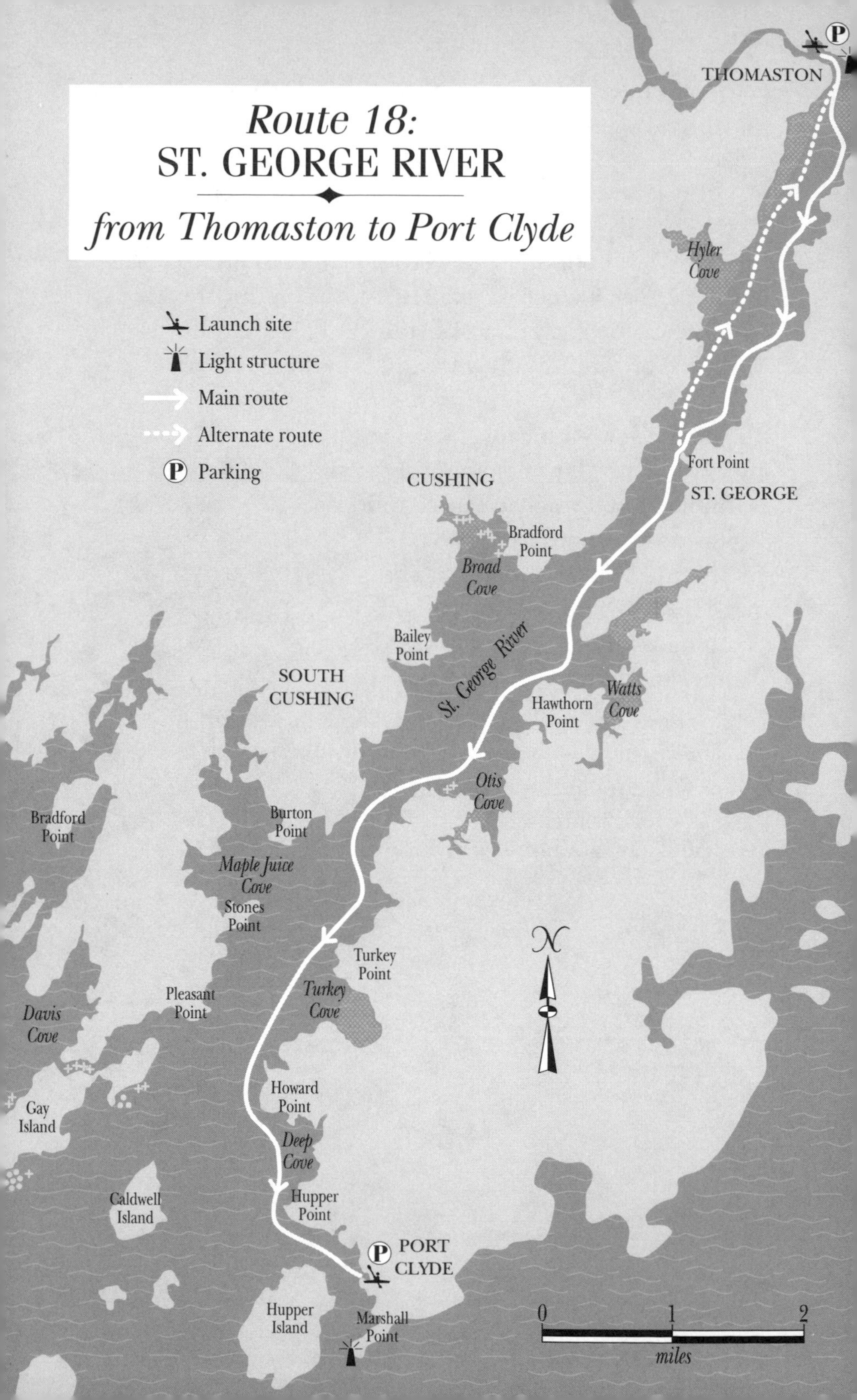
Route 18:
ST. GEORGE RIVER
from Thomaston to Port Clyde
Launch site
Light structure
Main route
Alternate route
Parking
THOMASTON
Hyler Cove
Fort Point
ST. GEORGE
CUSHING
Bradford Point
Broad Cove
Bailey Point
St. George River
SOUTH CUSHING
Hawthorn Point
Watts Cove
Otis Cove
Bradford Point
Burton Point
Maple Juice Cove
Stones Point
Turkey Point
Turkey Cove
Pleasant Point
Davis Cove
Gay Island
Howard Point
Deep Cove
Caldwell Island
Hupper Point
PORT CLYDE
Hupper Island
Marshall Point
N
0
1
2
miles

TRIP DURATION/LENGTH: The point-to-point paddle between Thomaston and Port Clyde is about 11 miles. The out-and-back trip from Thomaston to Fort St. George is about 6.5 miles.

NAVIGATIONAL AIDS: 13301 Muscongus Bay (1:40,000). Light on approach to Thomaston; buoys at Howard Point and Channel Rock.

CAUTIONS: Winds funneling upriver and opposing the tidal current. Mudflats along both shores. Exposed conditions at Marshall Point.

LAUNCH SITE: The Thomaston launch site is all-tide with a new rest room facility, picnic tables, and lots of parking. The Port Clyde boat ramp (all-tide) has almost no parking, but you may arrange for parking through the Ocean House Hotel (207–372–6691) or the Monhegan-Thomaston Boat Line (207–372–8848). It is a short walk from these parking arrangements to the water. Please be efficient when loading or unloading at the boat ramp: This is an incredibly busy ramp, and working boats and a ferry are constantly coming and going. You'll find several restaurants and take-out food stands within easy walking distance of the Port Clyde boat ramp. The well-stocked Port Clyde General Store is adjacent to the ramp.

LOCAL ATTRACTIONS: Thomaston has several restaurants, some sandwich shops, and lots of intriguing shopping. Historic homes of sea captains and merchants line the shady streets in this interesting town. Port Clyde has long been a busy harbor and home to industries based on the sea's bounty. During its heyday several factories canned sardines, herring, lobsters, and clams; local schools of menhaden were used for fertilizer and oil. Port Clyde is still a fishing port with a thriving lobster trade. Nearby Marshall Point Lighthouse is open to the public and has a small museum.

Tenants Harbor
to Camden

Route 19

Tenants Harbor and Wheeler Bay

This area, just southwest of Muscle Ridge Channel, offers plenty of protection from a variety of wind directions and some gorgeous scenery. However, public access is limited to the put-in at Tenants Harbor and a half-tide or better launch spot off Spruce Head. Still, this is a very enjoyable paddle with lots of tucked-away spots that just beg to be explored.

If you prefer a placid trip with calm waters and little or no wind exposure, head out of the harbor and angle northeast at red nun #2. This will put you into Long Cove and the protection of a row of islands that runs from the harbor mouth to Clark Island. These are beautiful islands, all privately owned, that typically hold cormorants, several gull species, and blue herons along shores dotted with sea roses. A network of ledges is uncovered at low tide and may block passage between islands, but they offer tidal pools rich in mussels, periwinkles, and a beautiful collage of colors.

On the top half of the tide, you can explore well up into the fingers of Long Cove, which is exposed ledge and then mudflats at low tide. Then head south to round the point of Clark Island to access Wheeler Bay. (You could actually portage the gravel road that connects to Clark Island, but the paddle around is quite nice.) At all but low tide you can pick your way through the seaweed and mussel beds that are exposed between Seavey and Clark Islands, or try paddling to seaward of Seavey (unless there is a storm surge from the south or southeast). You can usually observe seals on Seavey Ledges, and there is a large osprey nest on

the eastern side of Clark Island. Guillemots dive and dodge
as you paddle throughout the area. Blue herons feed along
the mudflats and tidal pools.

Tucking up into Wheeler Bay and then circling behind
Elwell Island into Rackliff Bay makes for a nice loop trip
from Tenants Harbor. If it's low tide, you'll have fun finding
the entrance to Makertown Cove, a little sneak of water
marked by a buoyed radar reflector just off the northwest
end of Calf Island. If you're looking for a few more hours of
exploring, round the point of Rackliff Island and enter Seal
Harbor, which is true to its name. You can typically see seals

on Long Ledge and the ledges off Seal Island. From here you can look out to the southwest end of the Muscle Ridge Islands to Graffam Island just across the channel. To return to Tenants Harbor, you can paddle to the seaward side of Whitehead Island, which has a beautiful little lighthouse on its southeast shore. There's not much protection when you take this outside route, but it does offer great views to the southwest and Mosquito Head or due south to Metinic Island. You can quickly head for cover, if need be, while you pick your way back to Tenants Harbor. As you near the mouth to the harbor, you'll see the old lighthouse and marker on Southern Island alongside a new estate—an interesting juxtaposition of styles. Over your shoulder you can see Two Bush Light as it flashes red off in the distance.

TRIP HIGHLIGHTS: Beautiful scenery full of harbor seals and bird life.

TRIP DURATION/LENGTH: As much or as little as you wish. A loop trip to Wheeler Bay is around 7 miles; longer options can include Whitehead Island and exploring the backreaches of Long Cove for a full day of 12 or more miles. This trip, like many others, offers the reward of exploring the picturesque twists and turns of the coastline or of taking a more exposed seaward route for the big views out to the Atlantic.

NAVIGATIONAL AIDS: Chart 13301 Muscongus Bay (1:40,000). Lighted bell buoy off Southern Island; nun off Northern Island; Whitehead Light; can off Seavey Ledges.

CAUTIONS: Any route outside the protection of Long Cove or Clark Cove is exposed. Ledge breaks at Seavey and Norton Island Ledges.

LAUNCH SITE: The Tenants Harbor town boat ramp is by far the best launch site. This is an all-tide ramp with limited parking and portable toilet facilities just up the hill on the left at the small ball field. If the parking lot is full, you can drop your boats off and then park at the Odd Fellows Hall on Watts Avenue or at the town office. It's a short stroll down to the water. There is also a place to launch boats off the Spruce Head causeway, but only on the upper

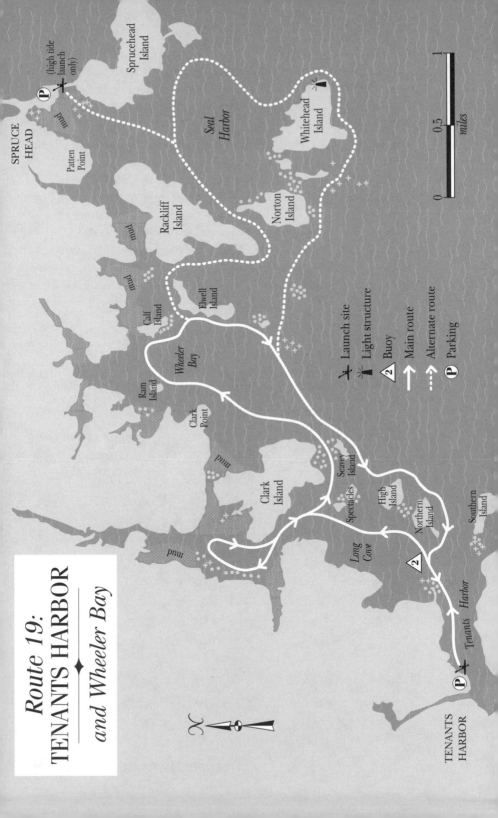

Route 19:
TENANTS HARBOR
◆
and Wheeler Bay

SPRUCE HEAD

P (high tide launch only)

Sprucehead Island

Spruce Island

Patten Point

mud

Seal Harbor

Whitehead Island

Rackliff Island

mud

Norton Island

mud

Calf Island

Elwell Island

Wheeler Bay

Ram Island

Clark Point

Clark Island

mud

Seavey Island

Spectacles

High Island

Northern Island

Long Cove

Southern Island

mud

Tenants Harbor

P

TENANTS HARBOR

✈ Launch site
⌖ Light structure
△2 Buoy
⬆ Main route
⇢ Alternate route
P Parking

0   0.5   1

miles

half of the tide. You'll also find some parking along the road.

Tenants Harbor straddles Route 131, which continues on to Port Clyde. You can access Route 131 from Route 1 between Rockland and Thomaston. Tenants Harbor is less than 10 miles down Route 131.

LOCAL ATTRACTIONS: Tenants Harbor is a pretty town with few of the tourist shops that crowd the sidewalks of Camden and Boothbay Harbor. There is the East Wind Inn (207–372–6366), with nicely appointed rooms and a restaurant, or try the Harbor View Guest House (207–372–8162). You can pack a lunch or snack from the Schoolhouse Bakery, or finish off the day at the Cod End, adjacent to the boat ramp. There is a grocery store just south of the turn to the boat ramp. Port Clyde, a short drive to the south, has its own restaurants and fresh seafood as well as boat service to Monhegan.

Route 20

Muscle Ridge Islands

The Muscle Ridge Islands sit only a couple of miles offshore, between Spruce Head and Ash Point. The islands were the site of several quarries, and communities thrived on some of the larger ones like Dix and Hewett during the latter half of the nineteenth century. There are no public islands in this area, so you'll need to provision accordingly. Since the water is shallow and calm on the interior of these islands, a kayak raft with sterns anchored within a mussel bed will make a fine picnic table and a stable platform to relax in without going ashore.

Seals are plentiful throughout this area and are easily observed: Simply sit still and keep a sharp eye out for their curious reconnaissance of your group. Be very careful to

avoid haul-out areas, especially during pupping season through May and June. The two most popular haul-out ledges are in the areas between Clam Ledges and the southern end of Dix Island, and between Hewett and Andrews Islands. If you see any seal activity, give these areas a wide berth.

Ospreys abound in the area, and you can spot their unruly nests on Birch and Great Pond Islands. During the summer months large rafts of eiders cruise the area and numerous shorebirds frequent the half-tide ledges. The area is rich in wildlife and a fertile site for lobsters and mussels.

The channel between this island group and the mainland, Muscle Ridge Channel, runs along a southwest–northeast axis and is easily crossed by kayaks. The tidal current can be a bit more than 2 knots, but with such a large target, it's easy to set a ferry angle as you cross from the beach at Birch Point to the island group. There are plenty of navigational buoys in the area, and by using the day beacons marking Otter Ledge and Otter Island, you can set up for a short hop across to the northeast end of the island group. A strong southwest wind opposing an ebbing tide can create very choppy conditions, so plan accordingly.

Once inside the island group, you can explore the ledges, small coves, and pocket beaches with lots of protection from the wind. The exposed side of the group can be dicey following a storm to the south, but there are lots of spots to duck back into for protection from the wind or storm surge. If the conditions are calm, you can hug the island shorelines where quarried blocks still sit at the water's edge. Yellow Ledge and Hewett Island Rocks can produce some nasty ledge breaks, so give yourself plenty of room as you paddle in this area. Even though the chart shows a spot of blue between the two halves of Hewett Island, plan on paddling around to explore the quiet cove and the remains of a fishing vessel that was grounded out long ago.

Muscle Ridge Islands

Keep an eye out for fog, which often moves into the area from the south. You'll need to beat a quick retreat back to Birch Point Beach or be confident in your bearings and reading of the tidal current and wind. If there is decent visibility, you can target a house with a red roof that sits on the cove just northeast of the beach where you started when you get ready for your return crossing. Since many sailing vessels motor through this channel in the fog, keep a sharp eye and ear out during any crossing. Remember that the marked channel is quite narrow for these boats.

If it's foggy or windier than you care to deal with during the crossing, consider paddling along the shoreline to the Weskeag River. A lot of area is inaccessible during low tide and there's a bit of current, especially during the middle of the ebb tide, but this spot is very protected from the wind and you'll find it easy enough to stay found in the fog. There is a sizable drop and standing waves below the bridge at South Thomaston where you'll come to the public boat ramp, but you can avoid this by staying to the right as you go upriver (river left). You may also choose to continue hugging the mainland shore and head southwest from Birch Point toward Spruce Head for a pleasant out-and-back trip.

Muscle Ridge Islands

TRIP HIGHLIGHTS: A cluster of islands teeming with harbor seals, eiders, and ospreys.

TRIP DURATION/LENGTH: This is a half- to a full-day paddle, depending on your curiosity and the conditions. The rocks at either end of the mainland beach are a great spot to warm up from a chilly paddle and enjoy a sunset repast.

NAVIGATIONAL AIDS: Chart 13305 Penobscot Bay (1:40,000). Day beacons at Otter Ledge and Otter Island.

CAUTIONS: Fog, boat traffic, and exposed conditions crossing Muscle Ridge Channel.

LAUNCH SITE: By the far the best site to launch from is Birch Point Beach. This is state-owned property and has ample parking, picnic facilities, and privies. Head out of Rockland on Route 73 and follow the signs to the airport. After you pass the airport, take the first right-hand turn onto Dublin Road. Follow Dublin Road to the first left turn at Ballyhac Road. Go 1.4 miles to the park entrance on the left. Follow this dirt road to the parking lot. There are privies and picnic tables but no water or overnight parking or camping.

There is also a public boat ramp in South Thomaston on the Weskeag River just before you cross the Weskeag bridge (continue on Route 73 out of Rockland until you come to the parking lot and launch site just before the Weskeag bridge and across from the small store). And you'll find a place to put in kayaks on the Spruce Head causeway. You can only use this site on the upper half of the tide; parking is minimal and alongside the road. Continue through South Thomaston on Route 73 until you see the left-hand turn for Sprucehead Island. The put-in is on the right side, where the road crosses to the island.

LOCAL ATTRACTIONS: There's kayaker-friendly camping at the Lobster Buoy Campground (207–594–7546) in South Thomaston, or you can kick back at the Craignair Inn on Clark Island (207–594–7644) or Blue Lupine Bed and Breakfast at Waterman Beach (207–594–2673). Nearby Rockland and Thomaston offer additional lodging, restaurants, and a host of galleries and museums. Locals claim that the best lobster rolls in the state are available at Waterman's Beach Take-out.

Muscle Ridge Islands

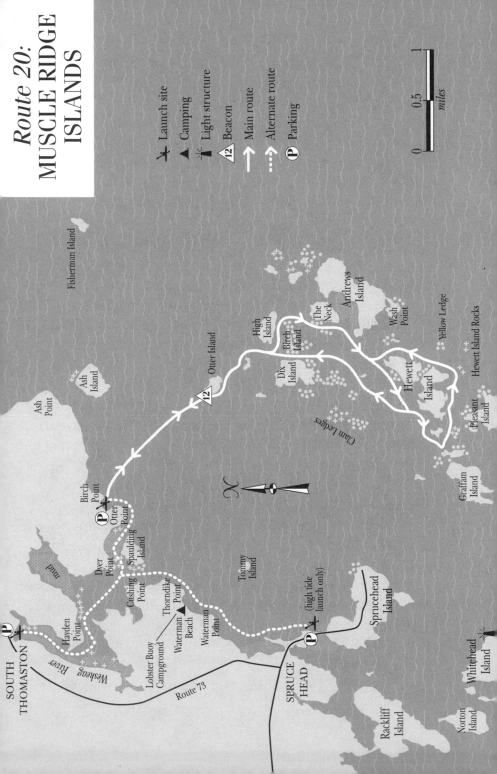

Route 20:
MUSCLE RIDGE ISLANDS

⟍ Launch site
▲ Camping
⟊ Light structure
△12 Beacon
↑ Main route
⇡ Alternate route
Ⓟ Parking

0   0.5   1
miles

Fisherman Island

Ash Point

Ash Island

Otter Island

High Island

The Neck

Andrews Island

Wash Point

Birch Island

Dix Island

Yellow Ledge

Hewett Island

Hewett Island Rocks

Clam Ledges

Pleasant Island

Graffam Island

Birch Point

Ⓟ Otter Point

Dyer Point

Spaulding Island

Cushing Point

Thorndike Point

Tommy Island

Waterman Point

Waterman Beach

Lobster Buoy Campground

Hayden Point

mud

Weskeag River

SOUTH THOMASTON

Ⓟ

Route 73

(high tide launch only)

Ⓟ

SPRUCE HEAD

Sprucehead Island

Whitehead Island

Norton Island

Rackliff Island

Route 21

-----------------------------➤

Rockport to Camden

Rockport and Camden offer what most chambers of commerce only dream about: picturesque villages arrayed around harbors that look out to islands and the blue expanse of open bay. Throw in a fascinating variety of sailing vessels, from newly minted yachts to proudly maintained windjammers, and the picture is enough to send a boat lover into ecstasy. The epicenter of midcoast Maine lies somewhere between these two towns, which are only a short distance apart as you cruise Route 1 (or sit in the traffic on a summer Friday). Having a kayak will allow you to see this shoreline from a unique vantage point beyond the reach of myriad ice cream stands and T-shirt vendors. Don't worry—they'll be there when you return. Sitting in either Rockport or Camden Harbor, you must choose whether to look back towards the village nestled against the hills or out to sea across the beautiful waters of Penobscot Bay.

Paddling along the shore between Rockport and Camden will also give you a close-up view of how new and old money is spent in America. There are stunning estates of weathered clapboard and wooded enclaves, as well as newer retreats with freshly planted landscaping. Leaving Rockport Harbor, you can paddle around Indian Island or pass between the island and Beauchamp Point for more wind protection. The lighthouse on Indian Island is no longer operable, and the island is privately owned and inaccessible to the public.

Along the shoreline, keep an eye out for any rebound

from Deadman Point. It's usually pretty tame, but a storm swell and sustained wind can kick things up a notch, so be aware of this piece of shoreline as you paddle northeast towards Camden. The Graves marks a point not quite halfway between the two harbors. This well-marked pile of rocks is of no concern to kayakers but a menace to large vessels that ply the shipping channel in this area. Hugging the shoreline is by far the most interesting, since the shallower waters shelter loons, cormorants (locally called shags), and an occasional harbor seal.

As you approach Camden Harbor, you'll want to head for Curtis Island, a town park and excellent picnic site. The island can be accessed from its northwest side. There is room to pull kayaks well up onto the shore before heading

up the access stairs. Consider paddling around the island first so you can get a good view of the lighthouse and the sea roses that blanket the southwestern shore. Once you're on the island, it's a short walk to the lighthouse, where you can spread out on the ledges. You may prefer to use the picnic table by the stairs on a windy day. A short trail meanders around the island's perimeter—it's a must. You'll usually see an osprey or two as you clamber along the northeast side. Seasonal caretakers now use the lightkeeper's house, and a small privy for public use is off to one side. Please respect the caretakers' privacy, and do not pick from their garden or enter their home.

Heading into Camden Harbor can often demand 360-degree vision. This is a busy harbor, but it's easy for a kayaker to get out of the way. Stay out of the entrance channel, which is clearly marked on the chart. If you want to explore the area to the northeast, cross the channel at a right angle and swiftly. This is not a place to park and take a picture. Camden Harbor is home to several vessels of Maine's windjammer fleet and to Wayfarer Marine, which has a railway on Eaton Point. The best time to see the windjammers is between Saturday afternoon and Monday morning when they reprovision for their next cruise.

The head of the harbor is marked with the long expanse of lawn that ends across Atlantic Avenue at the library and amphitheater. At high tide you won't be able to land here. You can tie up at the town dock, but this is often too crowded with dinghies. There is a public boat ramp on the northeast side of the harbor beyond Wayfarer Marine at the end of a row of condominiums. If you leave your kayak here for a walk into town, make sure it is pulled well up and off the ramp. Public rest rooms are available at the town landing but not at the boat ramp.

As an alternate route, you can always spend the

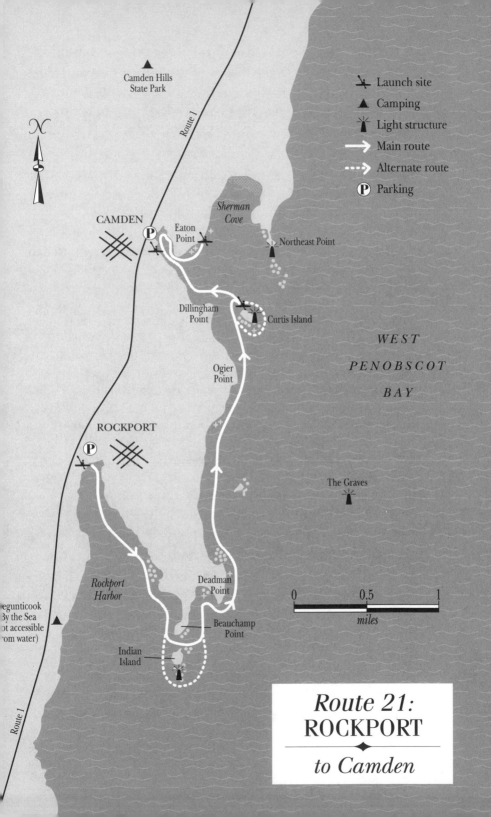

Camden Hills
State Park

N

CAMDEN

Eaton
Point

Sherman
Cove

Northeast Point

Dillingham
Point

Curtis Island

Ogier
Point

WEST

PENOBSCOT

BAY

ROCKPORT

*Rockport
Harbor*

Deadman
Point

The Graves

Beauchamp
Point

Indian
Island

egunticook
By the Sea
ot accessible
om water)

Route 1

Route 1

Launch site

Camping

Light structure

Main route

Alternate route

P Parking

0   0.5   1
miles

Route 21:
ROCKPORT

to Camden

afternoon exploring Camden Harbor and Curtis Island, which is often the better choice with kids. If there is a strong offshore breeze or thick fog, it might be best to head to Megunticook Lake just west of Camden for a pleasant, protected paddle.

TRIP HIGHLIGHTS: Traveling by kayak from one coastal village to another along some of the most expensive real estate in the state.

TRIP DURATION/LENGTH: This paddle from Rockport to Camden can be done as an out-and-back trip which is still a reasonable 9 miles in length. If you are fortunate enough to have a second car, you can leave it in Camden for an easy shuttle. But beware—finding a parking spot in Camden can be challenging. There are some decadent options for this trip: You can have a picnic lunch on Curtis Island, or spot a shuttle vehicle and plan a sunset paddle from Rockport to dinner at one of Camden's excellent restaurants. Generally, it is easiest to paddle from Rockport to Camden, because of the southwesterly sea breezes that begin to pick up around 11:00 A.M.; Curtis Island serves as your reward at the end of the trip. Also, the town of Camden has far more restaurants and other attractions if you want to explore from the land as well. However, it wouldn't be considered particularly contrary if you prefer to go the other way!

NAVIGATIONAL AIDS: Charts 13305 Penobscot Bay (1:40,000) and 13307 Camden, Rockport and Rockland Harbors (1:20,000). Seal Ledge beacon; the Graves; Curtis Island Light.

CAUTIONS: Strong winds and exposed conditions, especially around Deadman Point. Boat traffic in both harbors.

LAUNCH SITE: There is a public boat ramp in Rockport at the town's Marine Park, where you can park and launch for a small fee ($2). If you are coming from the south, turn right onto West Street at the elementary school across from the Market Basket (a great place for picnic supplies). At the end of West Street, turn left and look for the very sharp right-hand turn to the town landing. If you crossed the bridge over the Goose River, you missed it. From Camden, turn left onto Union Street at the blinking light at Village Variety and follow the road into Rockport. Cross the bridge over the Goose River and take an immediate left to the town landing. There is public parking and privies at the Marine Park.

LOCAL ATTRACTIONS: Numerous and varied! Try to plan a hike up Mount Battie (you could drive as well), which overlooks Camden Harbor and provides a spectacular view across Penobscot Bay. The entrance to the park is 2.3 miles north of Camden on Route 1. For lodging you have a full range of possibilities, from the time-warp quietness of Oakland Seashore Cabins (207–594–8104) to the personable Sign of the Unicorn Guest House (207–236–8789) on the Rockport side. In Camden, among numerous options, there is the convenient Lord Camden Inn (207–236–4200) and the award-winning Maine Stay Inn (207–236–9636). Camping is available at Camden Hills State Park (207–236–3109) or at the kayak-friendly Megunticook-by-the-Sea Campground (207–594–2428).

Lincolnville
Beach
to Stockton
Springs

Route 22

Saturday Cove to Warren Island

One of the reasons why we like this trip so much is the put-in at Saturday Cove: small, quiet, and very homey. Saturday Cove is just a slip of water below Bayside and Temple Heights. There's an old boat house and railway, and the pier is shaky at best. But it's easy to launch, and the site itself makes a nice picnic spot with its rope swing and cool shade in the summer. Launching from Saturday Cove also cuts down on your crossing mileage for a hop over to Warren Island State Park, which sits just south of Grindel Point off Islesboro. Warren Island has some short hiking trails that connect overnight shelters and picnic areas as well as privies and potable fresh water at the hand pump in its interior.

The crossing to Ram and Seal Islands is well over a mile. Don't dally: You'll be out into the main shipping channel that runs through western Penobscot Bay. The crossing will expose you to any seas running down the deep-water channel, as well as southwesterly and northeasterly wind directions. Set a ferry angle appropriate to the wind direction for your crossing so you don't fight the conditions any more than you'll need to during the crossing. If you are not comfortable with wind or wave exposure, this crossing should not be attempted. You are likely to be paddling in beam seas, or even following seas on the return leg. This is not the place for a capsize or for any tentative paddling. You may experience millpond conditions when you cross in the morning, only to be faced with a strong afternoon southwesterly that will have you rolling on beam or stern quarter seas all the way home.

If the crossing looks nasty in the morning or strong winds are predicted for the afternoon, you have the option of proceeding along the shore toward Belfast (north-northwest) or Lincolnville Beach (southwest). This shoreline is pleasant though it lacks many spots to tuck into for a break along the way—except for Ducktrap Harbor, a beautiful spot with a sandbar at its mouth just northeast of Lincolnville Beach. Both Lincolnville Beach and Belfast offer shopping and some good restaurants, with Belfast having more extensive offerings. You may prefer to spot another vehicle at one of these destinations unless you want to paddle the full out-and-back mileage, which can be a bit of a slog if the wind comes up. The hills along Temple Heights and Bayside offer little refuge if you are heading to Belfast.

TRIP HIGHLIGHTS: The exhilaration of paddling off shore to explore the big, brawny islands in these waters.

TRIP DURATION/LENGTH: A round trip from Saturday Cove to

Warren Island is about 10 miles and offers plenty to explore along the way for more mileage, so a full day with the right conditions is a must for this trip. Exploring along the mainland shore in either direction from Saturday Cove is open ended. If you plan on paddling to Belfast, the mileage is slightly less than 6.5 miles one way; to Lincolnville Beach, it is about 4.5 miles one way.

NAVIGATIONAL AIDS: Chart 13309 Penobscot River (1:40,000). Lighted bell buoy off Warren Island; Grindel Point Light.

CAUTIONS: Very exposed conditions during the crossing, fog, and boat traffic.

LAUNCH SITE: Launch from Saturday Cove in the town of Northport, which sits on Route 1 not quite halfway between Lincolnville Beach and Belfast. At the Saturday Cove Gallery on Route 1, you'll see Shore Road, which angles off the eastern side of

Saturday Cove to Warren Island

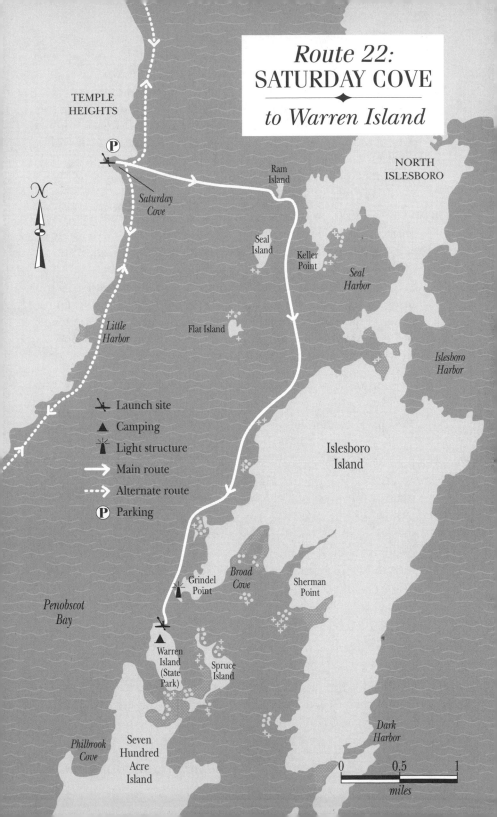

Route 22:
SATURDAY COVE
to Warren Island

TEMPLE
HEIGHTS

Ⓟ

Saturday
Cove

RAM
Island

NORTH
ISLESBORO

Seal
Island

Keller
Point

Seal
Harbor

Little
Harbor

Flat Island

Islesboro
Harbor

⚓ Launch site

▲ Camping

☼ Light structure

→ Main route

⇢ Alternate route

Ⓟ Parking

Islesboro
Island

Grindel
Point

Broad
Cove

Sherman
Point

Penobscot
Bay

Warren
Island
(State
Park)

Spruce
Island

Philbrook
Cove

Seven
Hundred
Acre
Island

Dark
Harbor

0   0.5   1

miles

Route 1. There is a blue PUBLIC LANDING sign at this turn. Proceed down Shore Road a short distance to a small intersection with another PUBLIC LANDING sign. The turn to the landing is straight ahead about 0.1 mile on your right. Parking is limited along the right side of the cove. If you are coming from the north, you may choose to access Shore Road from a point just south of the Little River bridge at Dos Amigos Restaurant. Follow Shore Road as it meanders through Bayside and Temple Heights and drops to Saturday Cove after a little more than 4 miles.

LOCAL ATTRACTIONS: Temple Heights, a spiritual camp, is just north of Saturday Cove. You can receive spiritual consultations and palm readings during some summer evenings (207–338–3029). The town of Bayside has no facilities but offers many seasonal rentals; it's a fascinating hodgepodge of cottage styles perched along the bluffs above the water. Dos Amigos Mexican Restaurant, located at the northern end of Shore Road, makes for a relaxing end to a paddling day, and nearby Belfast has numerous options for lodging, restaurants, and shopping.

Saturday Cove to Warren Island

Route 23

![arrow]

Belfast to Moose Point

From the bustling harbor of Belfast, you can observe the myriad activities of the town's waterfront. This is a working town overlaid with tourist amenities and a Main Street that is often pure funky. You can watch well-maintained tugs come and go as they shepherd tankers to their berths in Bucksport and a restored steamship take on a load of passengers for a cruise around the bay. You'll certainly get a whiff of the sardine factory that sits just north of the town dock, and you may also detect the smell of new money brought into town by credit-card giant MBNA.

From the put-in you can head up the Passagassawakeag River (locals call it "the Passy") through rolling hills dotted with small farms and a few newer homes. Once you're beyond the Route 1 bridge, you're in for a quiet, pleasant paddle as you work the tide toward the town of Brooks some 3 miles away. You might be surprised by the whistle from the scenic railroad's steam engine, which runs on the west side of the river during the summer months.

The tidal current, while detectable, doesn't make this a one-way thoroughfare. However, you'll appreciate the lazy run you can have when you plan to use the current in your favor. A strong northwesterly wind (these often move in following a cold front) can funnel down the river and stop you in your tracks; this is not a breeze you want to contend with for a paddle towards Moose Point, either. Southeasterly winds will make your return leg to the harbor a chore, but you are well protected from the building afternoon sea breezes out of the southwest as you paddle the Passy.

From Belfast Harbor you can also cross the widening river and head east and along the shoreline towards Searsport, with the "Monument" marking the outer harbor's entrance off Patterson Point to your right. The shoreline is wooded and quiet even though Route 1 traffic runs a short distance away. Moose Point, a small state park with picnic facilities and walking trails, pokes out from the shoreline about 2.5 miles from the town ramp. You can see the cobble beach and parking lot from the water. The best place to pull out is beyond the parking area just on the other side of the point. This makes a nice lunch spot. You can lounge in the sun before continuing your day of exploring.

As you round Moose Point, you'll see the white oil tanks on Mack Point to the northeast. This is a busy terminal for the large ships that ply the shipping channel off this piece of shoreline. You can continue paddling along these shores, but there is nothing particularly remarkable to see other than the industry at Mack Point and Sears Island, which is connected to the mainland by a causeway.

TRIP HIGHLIGHTS: A pleasant tidal run through farmland or along an accessible stretch of coastline.

TRIP DURATION/LENGTH: The round trip up the Passy and back is a bit less than 6 miles, which is nearly identical to the round-trip mileage from Belfast to Moose Point and back. Either of these choices makes a nice half-day trip, or you can combine the two for a full day. Ideally, you'll catch the tail end of the flood tide as you begin your river paddling. This will give an easier ride on the return.

NAVIGATIONAL AIDS: Chart 13309 Penobscot River (1:40,000). Steels Ledge Light.

CAUTIONS: Wind funneling up or down the river, exposed conditions along the shoreline to Moose Point. Boat traffic in Belfast Harbor.

LAUNCH SITE: Belfast sits just off the junction of Route 3 and

Belfast to Moose Point

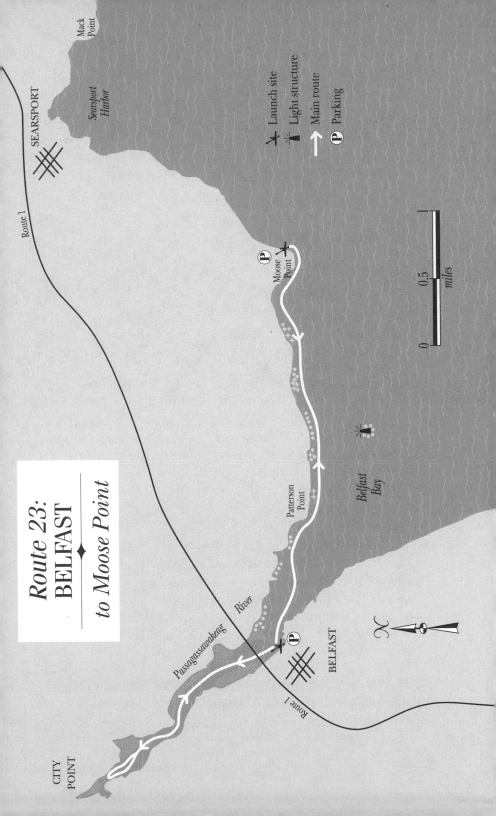

Route 23:
BELFAST
◆
to Moose Point

Mack
Point

SEARSPORT

Searsport
Harbor

Route 1

✝ Launch site
✳ Light structure
⬆ Main route
Ⓟ Parking

Moose
Point

☉ 0.5 1
miles

Patterson
Point

Belfast
Bay

Passagassawakeag
River

BELFAST

Route 1

CITY
POINT

Route 1. Follow the signs to downtown and the waterfront. Main Street and all the streets that empty into it flow gently down the hill towards the town dock. The town ramp is very busy, and there is a lot of commercial activity. Be ready to unload and then move your car to the town lot a short distance up the hill and on your right. Main Street parking is usually posted with two-hour limits, but the municipal lot allows all-day parking.

LOCAL ATTRACTIONS: The Belfast Food Co-op is on High Street just behind the southwest side of Main Street. It offers a wonderful variety of fresh produce, breads, and deli items for a fine picnic lunch. There's plenty of interesting shopping along Main Street, and the Belfast and Moosehead Lake Railroad (207–338–2330) leaves from the waterfront just to the left of the town ramp. For lodging in town, there's The Jeweled Turret Inn (207–338–2304), The Thomas Pitcher House (207–338–6454) or The Alden House (207–338–2151). The Comfort Inn (207–338–2090) and Belfast Harbor Inn (207–338–2740) are just across the river on Route 1.

Route 24

Fort Point (Penobscot River)

his pleasant trip can include exploring Fort Point State Park on foot and a picnic. Fort Point State Park is a well-maintained site at the eastern end of Cape Jellison adjacent to Stockton Springs. Fort Pownall, which dates from 1759, once sat on the site of the present state park as it guarded the entrance to the Penobscot River. There are some earthworks and foundation sites in the park, with interpretive signs as well as a lighthouse and signal bell. This makes a particularly good trip with kids, because you can keep the paddling legs short to leave lots of picnic and running-around time on land if needed. There are picnic tables and pit toilets close to a large pier on the north side of the point where you can land a sea kayak. There's plenty of room to pull boats up and out of the weather, and this is a fairly secure area to leave the boats for an afternoon of hiking. Please note that the cliffs along Fort Point below the lighthouse are steep and unguarded in some areas. Small children should be kept very close.

The paddle from the Sandy Point launch site is easy; you can hug the shoreline in low visibility. Shortly after your launch at Sandy Point, you'll see the old pilings of Steamboat Wharf, which used to serve traffic along the Penobscot River to Bangor. A strong southerly wind can make this trip a bit of a slog, but you can duck into Devereaux Cove and then continue to use land features for protection along the way. If you prefer, you can cut your mileage by paddling across Fort Point Cove for a direct route to the pier at the state park.

Be careful if you wish to round the point and explore along the southern shore of Cape Jellison. The current can be swift, and the shoals between green can #1 and Fort Point can be very tricky. Once you round the point, there is a nice view towards Islesboro, Castine, and the expanse of Penobscot Bay all the way to the Camden Hills. The lighthouse on the cliffs just around the point is a definite photo opportunity.

TRIP HIGHLIGHTS: Storming Fort Pownall by kayak and exploring Fort Point State Park.

TRIP DURATION/LENGTH: A paddle along the shoreline from Sandy Point to the state park pier and back is approximately 8 miles. A hike along park trails can make this a full day's outing. If

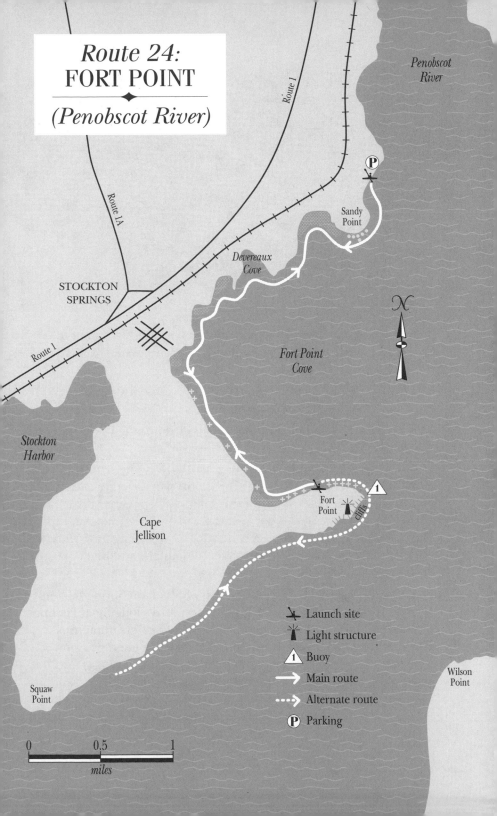

Route 24:
FORT POINT
(Penobscot River)

Penobscot River

Route 1

Route 1A

Route 1

STOCKTON SPRINGS

Sandy Point

Devereaux Cove

Fort Point Cove

Stockton Harbor

Fort Point

cliffs

Cape Jellison

Squaw Point

Wilson Point

N

Launch site
Light structure
Buoy
Main route
Alternate route
Parking

0   0.5   1

miles

you prefer, forgo the hike and continue around the point to explore the shores of Cape Jellison before returning to the park for a leg stretch and pit stop.

NAVIGATIONAL AIDS: Chart 13309 Penobscot River (1:40,000). Sandy Point buoy; can buoy off Fort Point; Fort Point Light.

CAUTIONS: Strong winds funneling up or down the river and challenging currents around Fort Point.

LAUNCH SITE: If you are heading north on Route 1 from Belfast, continue on Route 1 towards Bucksport when it splits with Route 1A. About 3.5 miles north of this intersection, there will be a right-hand turn onto Steamboat Wharf Road. Follow this downhill until you come to Sandy Point, a swimming beach with ample parking. This makes an easy site from which to launch into the Penobscot River.

LOCAL ATTRACTIONS: The town of Stockton Springs is home to several potters and other artisans, and there's lodging at Hichborn Inn (207–567–4183). Farther south, Belfast offers numerous shopping and lodging possibilities. Belfast is a good place to restock provisions at the Shop 'N Save (just off Route 1) and the Belfast Co-op (in town on High Street). A scenic railroad and a steamboat operate out of Belfast. The community of Temple Heights, where the mystical arts are alive and well, is just south of town.

Fort Point (Penobscot River)

Castine *to* Blue Hill

Route 25

Holbrook Island

Sitting just south of Dice Head and Castine Harbor, the Holbrook Island Sanctuary is a unique site that offers island access and mainland foot trails for hours of exploring. The sanctuary protects a total of 1,350 acres, including the 115-acre Holbrook Island. These lands were donated to the state by Anita Harris "to preserve for the future a piece of unspoiled Maine that we used to know." The mainland facilities include picnic tables, a pit toilet, a small parking area, and two beaches where kayaks can be launched easily.

These sites are managed by the Bureau of Parks and Lands with volunteer support from Friends of Holbrook Island Sanctuary. Ram Island, which sits just east of Holbrook, is managed by the local land trust and is open to limited day use (no fires!). Launch into Smith Cove from the sanctuary on the Cape Rosier mainland and explore this well-protected area as you meander through the small islands just across from the town of Castine. At low tide you'll have to swing outside this island group, but at half tide or better you'll have plenty of water for hours of enjoyable paddling. The channel leading from Dice Head into Castine is well marked, and as you round Nautilus Island, you'll see the larger Holbrook Island to the south. Castine Harbor offers a glimpse of the many yachts that visit its popular harbor and the Maine Maritime Academy training vessel, *State of Maine*. At Dice Head you can see both the abandoned lighthouse tower and the newer Coast Guard installation that sits just below it.

There are several places to land on Holbrook: a fairly
large beach on the northern side and other pocket beaches
along the eastern edge. The approaches to some of these
pockets are covered with mussels, and great blue herons
often feed along these shores. Kayakers may land on the
island and explore along the shores, but no camping and
no fires are allowed at any time. It's a great place for a
picnic, bird-watching, or just relaxing in the sun. Nearby
Ram Island can be explored from the knife-edge bar that
connects the two pieces of the island but shouldn't be
trusted as a place to park a kayak on a spring high tide.

Circumnavigating Holbrook Island makes for a
pleasant paddle. It's worth a few extra strokes to check out
Goose Falls just off the southeast end of the island. This
mainland site is a frothy spill of water from Goose Pond into
a small pocket harbor. You can continue to explore along
the western edge of Cape Rosier as far as you feel

comfortable. If it's a clear day, you can see Islesboro and the Camden Hills off to the west from just about any point throughout your explorations.

You may choose to simply backtrack to your launch site into Smith Cove or you may land on the beach directly across from Ram Island and portage your kayak along the short trail that connects the two park beaches. It's an easy walk; a kayak cart makes it a piece of cake. Please note that the area to the north of the park boundary is private property and should not be disturbed. A small fence and signs mark the boundary. When you are loading or unloading your kayak from your vehicle, you can temporarily park close to the beach, but you must move the vehicle back to the designated parking area further up the hill once you are done. Trail maps and a checklist of birds are available at the parking area, along with a spot to deposit your user fee ($1.00 per person).

TRIP HIGHLIGHTS: Picturesque harbors, sweeping views across the bay, and a unique island sanctuary.

TRIP DURATION/LENGTH: Mileage can vary from a mere 3-mile paddle to Holbrook Island and return by way of the beach portage trail, to as many miles as you feel like while you explore around this island group and the western shore of Cape Rosier. Smith Cove offers several hours of exploring and bird-watching along its shores. You may choose to paddle to the Castine Harbor dock and pull your kayaks out for lunch and a hike around the town's many historic homes and sites, with their interpretive signs.

NAVIGATIONAL AIDS: Chart 13309 Penobscot River (1:40,000). Nun buoy at Smith Cove; Hosmer Ledge day beacon; can buoy at Nautilus Rock; Dice Head Light.

CAUTIONS: Rebounding waves along Dice Head and exposed conditions south of Holbrook Island. A profusion of barred islands in the cluster off the harbor can make things interesting around low tide.

LAUNCH SITE: The Holbrook Island Sanctuary beach launches

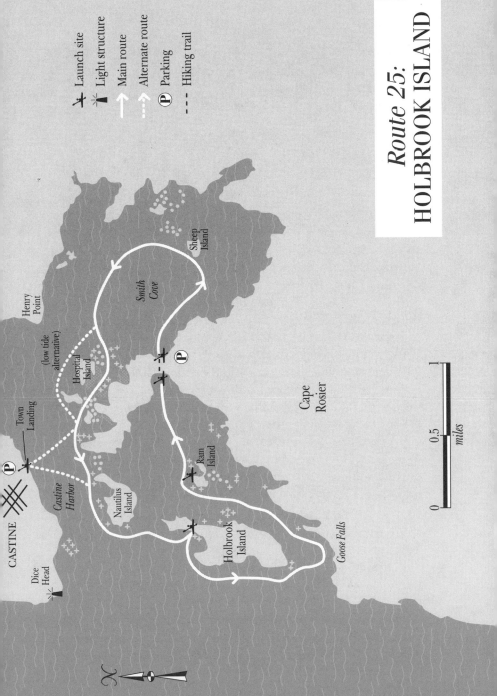

Route 25:
HOLBROOK ISLAND

Legend

- ✈ Launch site
- ☀ Light structure
- ⬆ Main route
- ⬆ Alternate route
- Ⓟ Parking
- - - Hiking trail

CASTLE

Dice Head

Ⓟ

Castine Harbor

Town Landing

Henry Point

(low tide alternative)

Hospital Island

Smith Cove

Sheep Island

Ⓟ

Nautilus Island

Ram Island

Holbrook Island

Cape Rosier

Goose Falls

miles
0   0.5   1

you into Smith Cove and is quiet and well protected. The area is
remarkably uncrowded, and the drive into the area is beautiful,
though a bit narrow and rough. After you cross the Bagaduce River
on Route 175/176, continue on Route 176 through North and
then West Brooksville. Turn right onto Cape Rosier Road at the
sign for the Holbrook Island Sanctuary. Continue for a bit more
than 1.5 miles and turn right onto Back Road where you see
another sanctuary sign. Go about 0.8 mile and turn right onto
Indian Bar Road, which meanders through the sanctuary woods to
the park headquarters and parking area. The beach is down the
hill from the parking area.

You may also launch from nearby Castine Harbor, where
there is a public dock, but it is busy and often crowded, especially
during summer weekends. You'll need to unload and then find
parking elsewhere, since the public lot has a two-hour limit.

LOCAL ATTRACTIONS: Numerous hiking trails in the sanctuary
range from 0.6 mile to 7.0 miles in length. Nearby Castine beckons
with waterfront pubs like Dennett's Wharf and unique lodging
establishments like The Pentagoet Inn (207–326–8616), Castine
Harbor Lodge (207–326–4335) and The Castine Inn
(207–326–4365). The area is rich in history and proud of it. The
second weekend in July sees the town inundated with sea kayakers
attending the L .L. Bean Atlantic Coast Sea Kayak Symposium held
at the Maine Maritime Academy and Wadsworth Cove, the town
beach between Perkins and Blockhouse Points.

Route 26

Eggemoggin Reach

The Reach is an impressive stretch of water that runs northwest–southeast from Cape Rosier to Naskeag Point. You'll find very few places to pull out in the Reach itself, except for several islands at its southeastern end. But there's plenty to explore along its shores on either side, and it's well worth the effort. These waters are notorious for funneling wind that can puff and gust and make it tough going for small boats. If winds from either the northwest or southeast are in the forecast, you'd be better off paddling elsewhere that day unless you're fond of hard work. The tidal current—which isn't particularly strong—floods northwest and ebbs southeast.

Exploring the northwestern end of the Reach starts from the facilities at Eggemoggin Landing just across the bridge on Little Deer Isle. From this launch site you can paddle the shores of Little Deer Isle and circle Pumpkin Island (private property) with its now-extinguished lighthouse, or continue on to Pond Island off Cape Rosier, where you may land along the middle stretches and explore its stretch of gravel beach. Please note that Pond Island is also home to nesting seabirds on either end of its length. These areas are closed from March 15 through July 15. The crossing to Pond can be rough in strong winds, especially from the south. You should consider making the nearly 1-mile crossing from Blake Point and ducking behind Spectacle Island if needed, rather than paddling on a westerly course from Little Deer Isle. Besides, there are some beautiful little coves along the southeast shore of Cape Rosier that deserve some attention.

Instead of paddling out to Pond Island, you may prefer to cross the Reach and explore up into Buck Harbor to the town of South Brooksville. You can usually land at Buck's Harbor Marine and pull your kayaks up onto the grass for a small fee and stretch your legs in town. The Buck Harbor Market (turn left from the dock and go a short distance to the market on the right) makes great sandwiches and is a nice place to hang out for a break from the water. You can continue to explore the many coves and fingers of water on the east side of Eggemoggin Reach before returning to Eggemoggin Landing. If you would rather hug the shoreline throughout the day, there's plenty to enjoy along the shoreline of Little Deer Isle for a pleasant out-and-back trip.

TRIP HIGHLIGHTS: Snug harbors and pocket coves that dot an impressive stretch of water.

TRIP DURATION/LENGTH: Paddling around Pumpkin Island is 5 miles round trip. From Pumpkin you can proceed to Buck's Harbor Marine (8 miles round trip) or on to Pond Island (12 miles round trip). The options are endless, since you can explore either shore along the Reach and could even head southeast down the Reach to explore in that direction.

NAVIGATIONAL AIDS: Chart 13309 Penobscot River (1:40,000). Buoys at the Triangles; lighted bell buoy at northwest end of Reach.

CAUTIONS: Puffy, gusty winds in the Reach that gain strength along a northwest–southeast axis. Very exposed conditions approaching Pond Island.

LAUNCH SITE: You can see the Eggemoggin Landing facilities as you come off the Deer Isle bridge on Route 15. At the base of the bridge, turn right into the parking lot and check in at the office to your left. This private site charges $3.00 to launch kayaks and $3.00 parking per day. The folks at Eggemoggin Landing will arrange a shuttle by advance reservation. There is just about everything here kayakers might need: restaurant, snack bar and ice cream stand,

Eggemoggin Reach

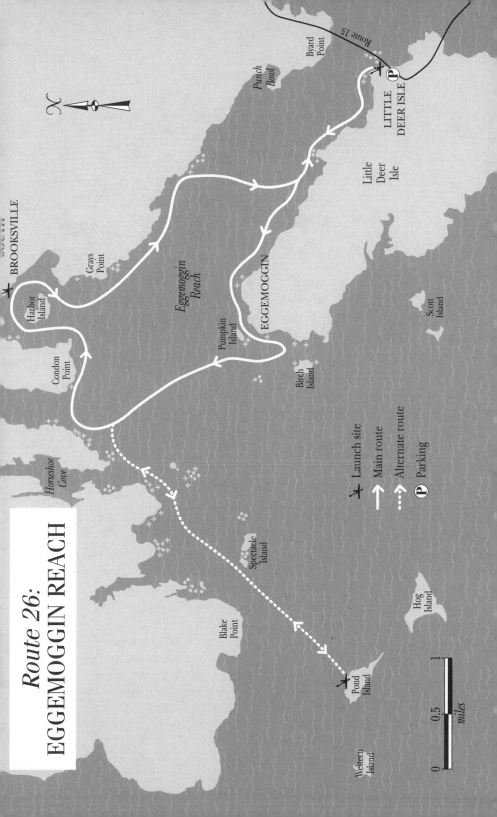

Route 26:
EGGEMOGGIN REACH

SOUTH
BROOKSVILLE

Harbor
Island

Condon
Point

Grays
Point

*Eggemoggin
Reach*

Pumpkin
Island

Horseshoe
Cove

Blake
Point

Spectacle
Island

Western
Island

Pond
Island

Hog
Island

Birch
Island

EGGEMOGGIN

Scott
Island

Little
Deer
Isle

Punch
Bowl

Byard
Point

LITTLE
DEER ISLE

Rowe 15

✈ Launch site
⬆ Main route
⬆ Alternate route
Ⓟ Parking

miles
0   0.5   1

picnic tables, fresh water, and a small motel. Kayakers often use this as a stop on a multiday trip around the Deer Isle area. For more information contact Eggemoggin Landing (207–348–6115 or www.acadia.net/eggland).

LOCAL ATTRACTIONS: There are many lodging establishments on both the mainland and Deer Isle side of the Reach. Several offer water access for kayakers but require minimum stays of three or more nights. The small towns of Brooksville, South Brooksville, and West Brooksville provide a variety of small bed-and-breakfast establishments like Buck's Harbor Inn (207–326–8660), or there's the rustic Oakland House and Shore Oaks Seaside Inn (207–359–8521) with its impressive grounds and waterfront location. You can cross the bridge to the Deer Isle peninsula to find small motels like the one at Eggemoggin Landing (207–348–6115). Both Blue Hill (on the mainland) and Stonington (on Deer Isle) are close by and offer a broad range of restaurants and facilities.

Route 27

Deer Isle Archipelago

The Deer Isle Archipelago offers the largest number of public-access islands and some of the best paddling on the Maine coast. The choices are often overwhelming—and the boat traffic and island use can be as well. The islands in this area are rounded and cracked granite topped with spruce trees; there are even meadows of wildflowers on the larger ones, like Harbor Island. Sea roses dot many of the shores. The "talking stone" beaches are a study in subtle hues and textures. The islands are more or less clustered, and all are within a reasonable day of paddling round trip from Stonington or Webb Cove.

The town of Stonington, which sits at the southern end of Deer Isle, is a popular launch site for multiday kayak trips, though there is something of an uneasy relationship between town residents and kayakers. Kayakers often use town facilities and crowd the launching sites and then depart without spending much at the local establishments. In addition, local lobstermen have voiced concerns about kayak visibility and safety in their local waters. Yet Stonington is still a prime destination for kayakers, and for good reason.

With the wealth of islands in this area, it is tempting to set out with no plans other than to meander at will and return at day's end. However, fog is prevalent in this area; it pays to plot courses and make plans and backup plans before launching. If your day starts out thick with fog, consider another activity. It's not worth being spooked by every sound of a nearby lobster boat or worrying about maintaining an accurate course in the absence of any landmarks.

A reasonable day of 12 miles' paddling will allow you to cruise in and out of islands with numerous stops along the way. You may land on the following islands: Weir, Hell's Half Acre, Steves, Wreck, Round, McGlathery, Harbor, Wheat, Little Sheep, and Doliver. All sit between Stonington and Isle au Haut to the south. You will most likely be joined on any of these islands by other day trippers, or by campers on the islands where overnight stays are permitted (Weir, Wheat, Harbor, Steves, Little Sheep, and Hell's Half Acre).

There are two boating channels that you should take special care in crossing: Merchant Row and Deer Isle Thorofare. The Thorofare is the channel that approaches the southern end of Deer Isle and Stonington from the west and east. Merchant Row lies further south and is the channel used by boats passing between Isle au Haut and

the cluster of islands off Stonington. Lobster boats, large cargo vessels, local powerboats, and a variety of sailboats of all sizes ply these waters. You'll need 360-degree vision at all times.

Note: while a glance at the chart shows that Isle au Haut is only about 5 miles out from Stonington, the actual National Park Service dock and landing site is at Duck Harbor on the southwestern shore. This makes the trip more than 8 miles of paddling one way, some of it quite exposed. A day trip to Isle au Haut should be considered only by strong and experienced paddlers with solid navigational skills who are willing to travel early and put in a long day. While the mileage alone is not overwhelming, the whole package that is needed to make this a safe trip may be more than most paddlers have.

TRIP HIGHLIGHTS: Beautiful islands of granite and fir are everywhere you look. This is a sea kayaker's paradise.

TRIP DURATION/LENGTH: Figure on paddling at least 6 miles if you want to get a feel for the islands in this area. Obviously, additional mileage will allow you to continue exploring or possibly reach some of the islands on the outer edge of Merchant Row, like

Harbor and Wheat. With all the available access, you shouldn't have any problems finding lunch stops or leg stretches along the way.

NAVIGATIONAL AIDS: Charts 13313 Approaches to Blue Hill Bay (1:40,000). Buoys along the Thorofare; buoys at Leach Rock, Harbor Island Ledges, and Bold Island Ledges; day beacon at Barter Island Ledges.

CAUTIONS: Fog and boat traffic. The crossing to Isle au Haut is exposed and can be difficult.

LAUNCH SITE: There are two launch sites in the town of Stonington: the town dock next to Bartlett's Market off Main Street (a bit high but still usable by kayakers), and the small ramp behind the ferry service building off Bayview Avenue. Neither site offers parking for the day and most parking in town has a designated two-hour limit. However, there are parking services available that fit the bill: Steve's Garage and Island Parking (207–367–5548; $5.00 per day) may be reached by following Main Street and turning right after the Opera House. Go up the steep hill past the old elementary school and continue for 0.12 mile to the road fork. Take the left fork for 0.25 mile; you'll see the sign, and should take the paved road on the left. Go another 0.25 mile to the lot in the field on the left. With advance notice, Steve's service will shuttle you back into town. You may also pay to park at the Isle au Haut Company on Seabreeze Avenue (207–367–5193 or 207–367–6516), where there is a fenced lot (you'll want to confirm at what time the gates are locked for the night).

Please note that the boat ramp behind the ferry service building is often crowded and in use by local fishermen, who need to get in and out quickly. Make your loading and unloading efficient, and move your vehicle out of the area immediately.

There is a much easier and more convenient launch site at Old Quarry Ocean Adventures (207–367–8977) on Buckmaster Neck. This business caters to kayakers. You'll find a small store with charts and all the last-minute gear you might need, shuttle service, a large boat ramp, a campground, a freshwater practice pond, shower and rest room facilities, a laundry room, and guide service. The staff will also file your float plan as a safety service and even provide island provisioning for multiday excursions. There is a $5.00-per-kayak launch fee and $5.00-per-day parking fee for use of

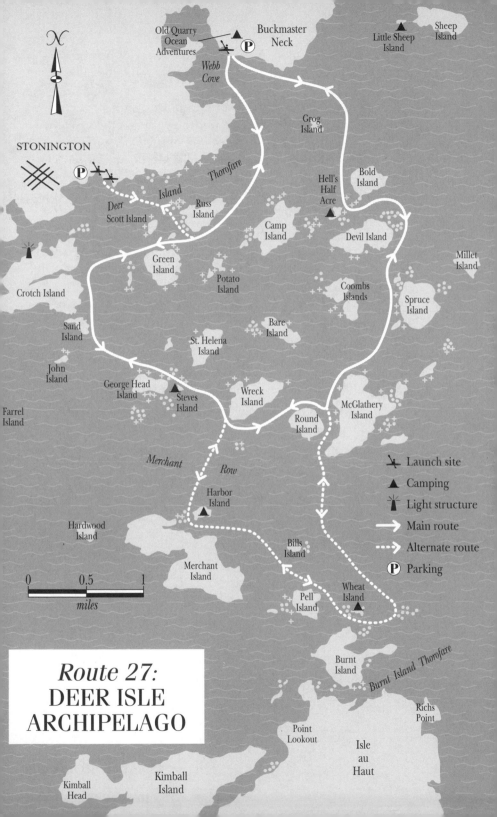

N

Old Quarry Ocean
Adventures
Buckmaster
Neck
△ P
☼
Little Sheep
Island
Sheep
Island
△

*Webb
Cove*

Grog
Island

Thorofare

Bold
Island

Hell's
Half
Acre
△

STONINGTON

P
☼
Island

*Deer
Scott Island*

Russ
Island

Devil Island

Millet
Island

Camp
Island

Green
Island

Potato
Island

Coombs
Islands

Spruce
Island

☼
Crotch Island

Bare
Island

Sand
Island

St. Helena
Island

John
Island

George Head
Island

Steves
Island △

Wreck
Island

McGlathery
Island

Farrel
Island

Round
Island

Merchant

Row

Harbor
Island △

Bills
Island

Hardwood
Island

Merchant
Island

Pell
Island

Wheat
Island △

	Launch site
▲	Camping
☼	Light structure
→	Main route
⇢	Alternate route
P	Parking

Burnt
Island

Burnt Island Thorofare

0   0.5   1
miles

**Route 27:
DEER ISLE
ARCHIPELAGO**

Point
Lookout

Isle
au
Haut

Richs
Point

Kimball
Head

Kimball
Island

their gravel ramp, which overlooks Webb Cove just northeast of Stonington. Launching from here adds a bit more mileage, but the convenience is unparalleled.

To reach Old Quarry Ocean Adventures, look for the KAYAK LAUNCH SITE sign at Ron's Garage on Route 15 and the Oceanville Road (9.7 miles from the southern end of the Deer Isle bridge). Proceed on Oceanville Road for 0.9 mile and turn right onto Fire Road 22, where there is another sign pointing the way. Proceed along this road through the Sunshine Seafood lot to the granite pillars marking the entrance to Old Quarry Ocean Adventures.

LOCAL ATTRACTIONS: Stonington offers a variety of small motels, inns, and bed-and-breakfast establishments. Other nearby towns like Deer Isle, Sunset, and Oceanville have lodging as well. You'll find several restaurants and lots of shopping along Stonington's Main Street. Bartlett's Market has all the provisions for a picnic, and there are plenty of ice cream vendors. If it's a foggy day, there are antiques shops and the Deer Isle Granite Museum on Main Street, which has a fascinating display of the quarry operations on nearby Crotch Island. Or you can hike the Island Heritage Trust's trails at Settlement Quarry. The trail begins at the small parking area at the Fire Road 22 turn off Oceanville Road.

Lobsters and Lobster Boats

While the course of a lobster boat working its string may look aimless, there really is a method to the madness. First of all, look at the housetop (roof of the pilothouse). You'll see on dsplay the exact buoy that belongs to that lobsterman. Now look around the immediate area and pick out all of those buoys that match. You may not know which direction the boat's heading, but you should at least have narrowed the choices a bit.

Each lobster boat has an easily discernible working side. Look for chafing gear and the worn-out, gouged side where the traps are pulled aboard before being checked and rebaited. Lobstermen will always work on this side of the boat, pulling and dropping gear as they move through their string. They will often move from one buoy to another without a glance at their nonworking side if they don't know you're there. Never approach a boat from its nonworking side. Try to predict which buoy will be approached next, and give the lobster boat a wide berth as you swing to one side. Better still, sit and enjoy what is an essential part of the Maine seascape.

There's also nothing wrong with hailing the lobsterman and buying lobsters fresh from the boat. Have a mesh bag handy to store them in and enough cash to round it up to the nearest five. Store the "bugs" in your boat (if they're in the cockpit, make sure they're in a bag!) and paddle to your picnic spot. Set up your camp stove and cover the bottom of a large cooking pot with about 2 inches of seawater. Throw in some seaweed and drop in the lobsters (remove the bands) when there's a full boil. Cover everything with more seaweed and some tinfoil or the cooking pot's lid. Cook only until they turn red and let them cool on a bed of seaweed while you find a small stone for shell cracking. Enjoy!

Route 28

Blue Hill

Exploring Blue Hill Harbor and the surrounding waters makes for a full day or afternoon of relaxed paddling in a relatively protected area. There are pleasant views in every direction, and the shoreline is nicely contoured and dotted with saltwater farms as well as newer getaways for the summer crowd. There are few places to pull out and not many islands in this area, but the town of Blue Hill is a great place to start and finish with its fine restaurants, art galleries, and nearby farmer's co-op market. A half-acre island, Twin Oaks, on the southern end of the inner harbor is open to the public for day use. If you are looking out the passage to the outer harbor, it is on your right before you reach the small pocket cove below Parker Point.

The inner harbor is very well protected, but you will need to paddle through a narrow channel to access the outer harbor, the waters of Morgan Bay, and the upper reaches of Blue Hill Bay. During the strongest run of the tide, this well-marked constriction produces a pretty stiff current that you'd do well to plan around. Paddling against it requires an all-out sprint, and you'll have constricted boat traffic to contend with as well. It's much easier to cruise through at calmer water, when you can hang to the edges to avoid other boaters.

There's some fun exploring along the shoreline to the south as you paddle along the edges of the outer harbor. You'll see Blue Hill Falls about 1.5 miles after exiting the inner harbor. The water pours under the Route 175 bridge into Salt Pond and creates a sizable standing wave on the

flood tide. This is a favorite play spot for white-water boaters and some swimmers, but it's too quick a run for sea kayaks, and the wave train is too tight for longer boats. The ebb tide creates some turbulence as well but isn't as popular with play boaters because there are too many obstacles and the eddy doesn't give quite the free ride to the top that it does on the flood tide. It is best for sea kayakers to paddle by, since there are no public landings in this area.

At this point you may choose to cross over to privately

held Long Island for some shoreline exploring or continue south and take a leg stretch at the South Blue Hill town ramp about 1.5 miles south of the falls. There aren't any facilities at this site, but you can land and take a break if needed. If you like the idea of circumnavigating Long Island, the South Blue Hill ramp makes a better launch site, since it cuts the mileage for the circumnavigation to a more manageable 12 miles.

You may also want to consider paddling along the mainland shoreline to the northeast after exiting Blue Hill Harbor. The town of East Blue Hill sits on McHeard Cove, a beautiful little cove that is quiet and feels well removed from the bustle of summer crowds. Adjacent to the boatyard facilities is a small town boat ramp where you can stretch your legs before continuing your explorations. The group of islands off Conary Point at the mouth of Morgan Bay are favorite seal haul-outs, so give them a wide berth and have your binoculars handy. Osprey are a common sight, and we have heard of bald eagles being spotted in this area as well.

TRIP HIGHLIGHTS: Beautiful villages, a reversing falls, and a pastoral stretch of coastline.

TRIP DURATION/LENGTH: You can make this a full day's or a pleasant afternoon's paddle, depending on your preferences. The trip from the Blue Hill town ramp past the falls with a turnaround at the South Blue Hill ramp is about 8.5 miles, but you can add miles by exploring a patch of Long Island's shoreline. The trip from the Blue Hill ramp to McHeard Cove and then around the ledges and islands off Conary Point is between 10 and 11 miles. Remember to time your entrance and exit from the inner harbor at Blue Hill to avoid the middle of the tide. Of course, you can simply hang out in the inner harbor for a relaxing paddle of a few hours and enjoy the town's amenities for the rest of your day.

NAVIGATIONAL AIDS: Chart 13316 Frenchman Bay and Mount Desert Island (1:40,000). Buoys at entrance to inner harbor (Blue Hill); nun buoy off South Ledge; Jim's Point buoy off Long Island.

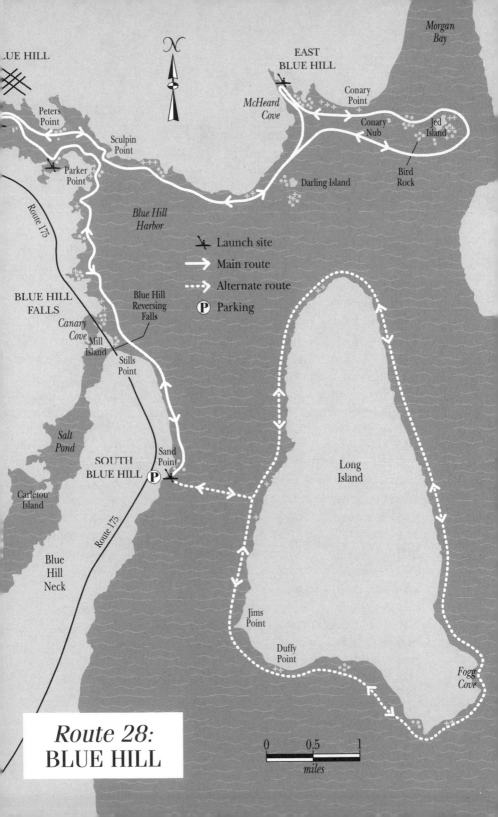

BLUE HILL

Peters
Point

Sculpin
Point

Parker
Point

*Blue Hill
Harbor*

EAST
BLUE HILL

*McHeard
Cove*

Conary
Point

Conary
Nub

*Morgan
Bay*

Jed
Island

Bird
Rock

Darling Island

Launch site

→ Main route

⇢ Alternate route

Ⓟ Parking

Route 175

BLUE HILL
FALLS

*Canary
Cove*

Mill
Island

Blue Hill
Reversing
Falls

Stills
Point

*Salt
Pond*

SOUTH
BLUE HILL

Sand
Point

Ⓟ

Route 175

Long
Island

*Carleton
Island*

Blue
Hill
Neck

Jims
Point

Duffy
Point

*Fogg
Cove*

Route 28:
BLUE HILL

0   0.5   1
miles

CAUTIONS: The reversing falls at the Route 175 bridge. Swift current at the mouth of the inner harbor. Wind and chop during a crossing to Long Island.

LAUNCH SITE: Route 15 is the main road through Blue Hill. The town boat ramp can be reached by driving through the hospital parking lot just off the main road or turning toward the water at the blue SHORE ACCESS sign just before the bridge if you are heading north. There is a small parking area and a concrete ramp that is best used at half tide or better. At less water than this, the area is very mucky.

There is a small parking area and a concrete ramp that is best used at half tide or better. At less water than this, the area is very mucky.

The South Blue Hill ramp can be reached from Route 175. Look for the PUBLIC BOAT ACCESS sign about 1.5 miles beyond the reversing falls if you are coming from the north. If you are traveling from the south, begin to keep a sharp eye out for the sign after you pass High Head Road on your right. If you pass Sand Point Road, you've missed it. The South Blue Hill ramp is a concrete, all-tide ramp with a small parking area.

LOCAL ATTRACTIONS: The town of Blue Hill offers a wealth of things to do and eat. There are summer chamber concerts at Kneisel Hall, and often open-air entertainment at the town park overlooking the harbor. Lodging options are plentiful and include the venerable Blue Hill Inn (207–374–2844) in the heart of Blue Hill, and the unique First Light Bed and Breakfast (207–374–5879) in East Blue Hill. After a day of paddling you can stroll down Main Street where the quality and range of restaurants is most impressive.

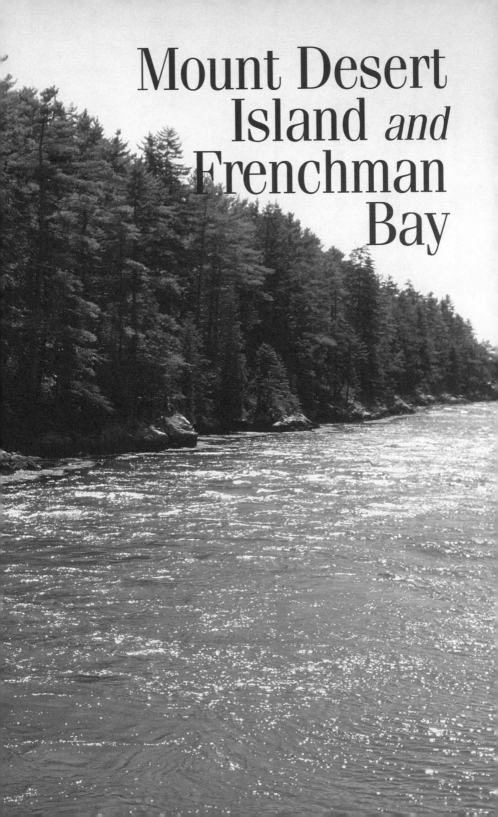

Mount Desert Island *and* Frenchman Bay

Route 29

------- ------- ------- ------- ------- ------- -------➤

Mount Desert Narrows

Mount Desert Narrows is the northern route that connects Blue Hill Bay, to the west, and Frenchman Bay, to the east. This channel passes under the Route 3 bridge between Trenton and Thompson Island, which is the only land route onto and off Mount Desert Island. There are two easy launch sites on Mount Desert Narrows: the Trenton ramp, adjacent to the Hancock County Airport, and Thompson Island. Both have large parking areas and some facilities, but the Thompson Island launch is not usable for two hours or so on either side of low tide. This area, rich in bird life, dries out to form mudflats that cover an extensive area.

There is a strong current running under the bridge at the channel's narrowest point during the middle of the tidal cycle, and you don't need to challenge it. The paddling throughout Eastern Bay offers plenty to explore, and access to Western Bay is easier from points to the west. The best exploring in Eastern Bay is along the Mount Desert shoreline, where the topography changes from mudflats to sandy to craggy along the paddling route. You'll be well protected from any strong southerly or northerly winds, but an occasional westerly wind may prove formidable as it funnels down the Narrows.

As you leave either the Trenton or Thompson Island launch site, you'll find an abundance of birds in the area around Thomas Bay, which feed along the mudflats and marsh, fed by freshwater streams. Ospreys, bald eagles, blue herons, and a variety of shorebirds and ducks can be found here and should be observed from a distance so they can feed undisturbed. (Do not land on the privately owned Thomas Island or The Twinnies.) About a mile beyond The Twinnies is Hadley Point, a pleasant sand beach that makes a fine leg stretch or picnic stop. This area is a popular site with easy access from Bar Harbor, and it's also a potential kayak launch site if needed.

Beyond Hadley Point the waterway opens up a bit. You can see Lamoine Beach and Lamoine State Park across the channel. The views to the south and the mountains of Mount Desert Island are spectacular, and the shoreline offers plenty of texture and contour to examine. You'll pass Emery and Salisbury Coves, which offer places to tuck into if the wind is of any consequence. Salisbury Cove is particularly pretty, though it is about half dry at low tide. Continue along the shoreline for another mile and you'll see a wonderful set of sea caves, the Ovens, just beyond Sand Point. The land along the shoreline is privately owned, so please do not ascend the stairs adjacent to the area.

You can walk among the sea caves and undercuts in the Ovens or poke your kayak up into them at high tide. These formations have been known to drop debris, and you can see the evidence of a rather sizable break that occurred in 1994, so keep a wary eye out. Cathedral Rock sports an eyehole that is too narrow for a kayak but may be walked through at low tide. These caves developed as the compressed volcanic ash that makes up this shoreline was eroded or cleaved along formation lines and fell into the water.

From the Ovens you can begin the return leg to your launch site at Thompson Island or Trenton, or continue to explore to Bar Harbor for a point-to-point trip.

TRIP HIGHLIGHTS: A great stretch of water rich in wildlife. Sea caves and views of the mountains of Mount Desert.

TRIP DURATION/LENGTH: The round-trip paddle from either the Trenton ramp or the Thompson Island put-in to the Ovens is between 9 and 10 miles, depending on whether you need to make any mudflat detours. With a stop at Hadley Point and nice break at the Ovens, you can easily spend the day exploring this area.

NAVIGATIONAL AIDS: Chart 13318 Frenchman Bay and Mount Desert Island (1:40,000). Googins Ledge buoy; Bar Harbor airport tower and light.

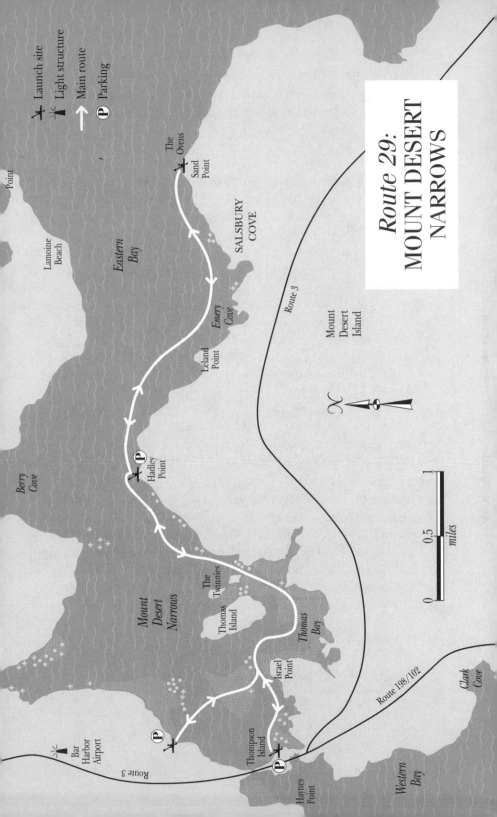

Route 29:
MOUNT DESERT NARROWS

Legend:
- ✈ Launch site
- ✖ Light structure
- ↑ Main route
- Ⓟ Parking

The Ovens

Sand Point

SALSBURY COVE

Eastern Bay

Lamoine Beach

Point

Emery Cove

Leland Point

Berry Cove

Hadley Point Ⓟ

Mount Desert Narrows

The Twinnies

Thomas Island

Thomas Bay

Israel Point

Thompson Island

Haynes Point Ⓟ

Route 3

Bar Harbor Airport

Western Bay

Route 198/102

Clark Cove

Route 3

Mount Desert Island

0   0.5   1
miles

CAUTIONS: Swift current at the Route 3 bridge. Mudflats on lower third of tide. A westerly breeze that funnels down the Narrows.

LAUNCH SITE: The Thompson Island picnic area is on your left just after you cross the Route 3 bridge heading east over the Mount Desert Narrows. There are rest room facilities and picnic tables at this popular site. It can get congested; plan your launch and landing to avoid the two hours on either side of low tide.

The Trenton boat ramp is wide and all-tide (they even launch seaplanes from here), and there's plenty of parking. As you approach Mount Desert Island along Route 3, you'll see Caruso Road (a left turn) and a sign for the Hancock County Airport. Proceed down this road for 0.3 mile and turn right at the sign for Able Custom Yachts. Follow this road down to the ramp and parking area.

The Hadley Point beach may be used if you need to shorten your paddling time to the Ovens, or if you want to split the difference and check out the Ovens and the shore along Bar Harbor on the same day. Off Route 3 turn onto Hadley Point Road, which is across from Rose Eden Cottages; there is a large sign for Hadley Point Campground. Continue down this road, which ends at the beach. Do not park in the sand unless you enjoy the stomach-churning sound of your tires spinning and the aftermath of that glorious event. You can expect this site to be crowded on a sunny summer day.

LOCAL ATTRACTIONS: This is the second most popular national park in the country and the most popular destination point in Maine, so plan on being overwhelmed with options and crowds during the summer months. Acadia National Park is a treasure with its restored carriage roads and spectacular scenery full of hiking trails, climbing spots, quiet ponds, mountain bike trails, campgrounds, and a wealth of wildlife. The town of Bar Harbor offers all the services even the most jaded tourist could demand.

Route 30

Bar Harbor and the Porcupines

While this trip may sound like a punk rock group, it's really a wonder of geology and incredible scenery. The Porcupines—Long, Burnt, Bald, and Sheep—sit just to the east of Bar Harbor and feature impressive and many-hued geological formations with fascinating shapes and textures that speak of glacial activity long ago. You'll definitely want to bring plenty of film for your camera: Every angle offers fresh views of these island shores, and a glance to the west places the historical rusticator mansions against a backdrop of the mountains. Numerous seabirds and shorebirds frequent this area, and harbor porpoises are common sights.

Everywhere you look you can see signs of glacial activity and lessons in geology. You'll spot erratics that dot the shore; fascinating layers of rock called the Bar Harbor formation, with streaks of white, reddish, and darker-hued rock; sea caves and jagged overhangs, where glaciers tore chunks from the bedrock; and an incredible variety of beach shapes and materials, from "popplestones" (local term for cobblestones, or rocks rounded smooth by wave action) to layered sand. Even the sloping shape of the islands as they rise from their southern to northern ends is a record of glacial movement and pressures. These are commonly called whalebacks and are noticeable throughout the area.

Conditions can change rapidly over the course of this paddle, so you'll need to remain flexible and be ready to head in early to seek shelter along the shoreline if needed. A strong northerly can build surprisingly nasty seas, and it is typical for southwesterly winds to gain strength through the early hours of the afternoon to roughen up the best-laid plans. The area around Rum Key (a privately owned island between Burnt and Long Porcupine) can be particularly rough if seas build on a strong southerly and oppose an ebbing tide. A planned loop around Long Porcupine may find you running for shelter from a southerly breeze and backtracking on the northern side to return home.

You can launch from the town ramp in Bar Harbor or from the rocky shore at Albert Meadows, which is just up and tucked off Main Street. Several islands in this area offer public access, but you'll want to make sure to give seabirds and other wildlife a wide berth, especially during the early-summer months when they are most vulnerable. Bar Island, which bars to the mainland at low tide, is often full of

tourists who stroll over for a look. The mud and sandbar is a favorite feeding spot for shorebirds when they aren't driven off by the people. Don't even consider trying to muck your way across the bar at full low tide; you're liable to leave your footwear behind in the sucking mud.

The islands of Sheep Porcupine, Bald Porcupine, and the Hop are part of Acadia National Park and are open to the public, though Sheep Porcupine is home to nesting seabirds and should be avoided until nesting season is over in early August. Long Porcupine, owned by The Nature Conservancy, is only open to day use after August 15. The cliffs of this island are home to nesting guillemots; other seabirds, bald eagles, and ospreys also nest on this protected island. The Hop is a small island that bars to Long Porcupine and makes an easy stop for a leg stretch or lunch. Treat it gently, however, because sensitive nesting sites are nearby. Burnt Porcupine is privately owned. Though paddlers regularly check out the keyhole on its western shore (do not enter except under flat calm conditions, and be willing to back out), please do not land on this island.

The channel between Sheep Porcupine and Burnt Porcupine is marked by green bell bouy #7. It's a busy route between the islands. Be very cautious about crossing this area in foggy conditions. In general, fog should keep you along the Mount Desert shoreline. You don't want to find yourself picking your way through the heavy boat traffic in these waters under a blanket of fog.

If you plan to visit Bald Porcupine Island, which is connected to the breakwater, you'll have to cross an open stretch of water where you'll be exposed to any wind or choppy seas. Beyond Bald Porcupine you can explore along the Mount Desert shoreline to Compass Harbor, which sits between Ogden and Dorr Points and makes a nice lunch stop or leg stretch. The shoreline along the cove and Dorr Point is owned by Acadia National Park and open to the public for day use.

TRIP HIGHLIGHTS: Incredible scenery that's a lesson in geology: cobblestone beaches, sea caves, overhangs, whalebacks, and glacial erratics.

TRIP DURATION/LENGTH: A paddle of a bit less than 13 miles will allow for a long loop around the eastern side of Long Porcupine and then a trip to Bald Porcupine and Compass Harbor. That said, weather conditions may well prevent a full loop, since there are open exposures to both the south and the north during portions of this trip and fog could halt your progress at any point. Instead, you may want to hug the Mount Desert shoreline down to Compass Harbor and beyond for a more protected paddle, using the land contours for protection and staying found as needed. Or if you are pressed for time, try just a jaunt around Bar Island or Sheep Porcupine.

NAVIGATION AIDS: Chart 13318 Frenchman Bay and Mount Desert Island (1:40,000). Bell buoy off Sheep Porcupine; Bar Harbor Light at the breakwater.

Bar Harbor and the Porcupines

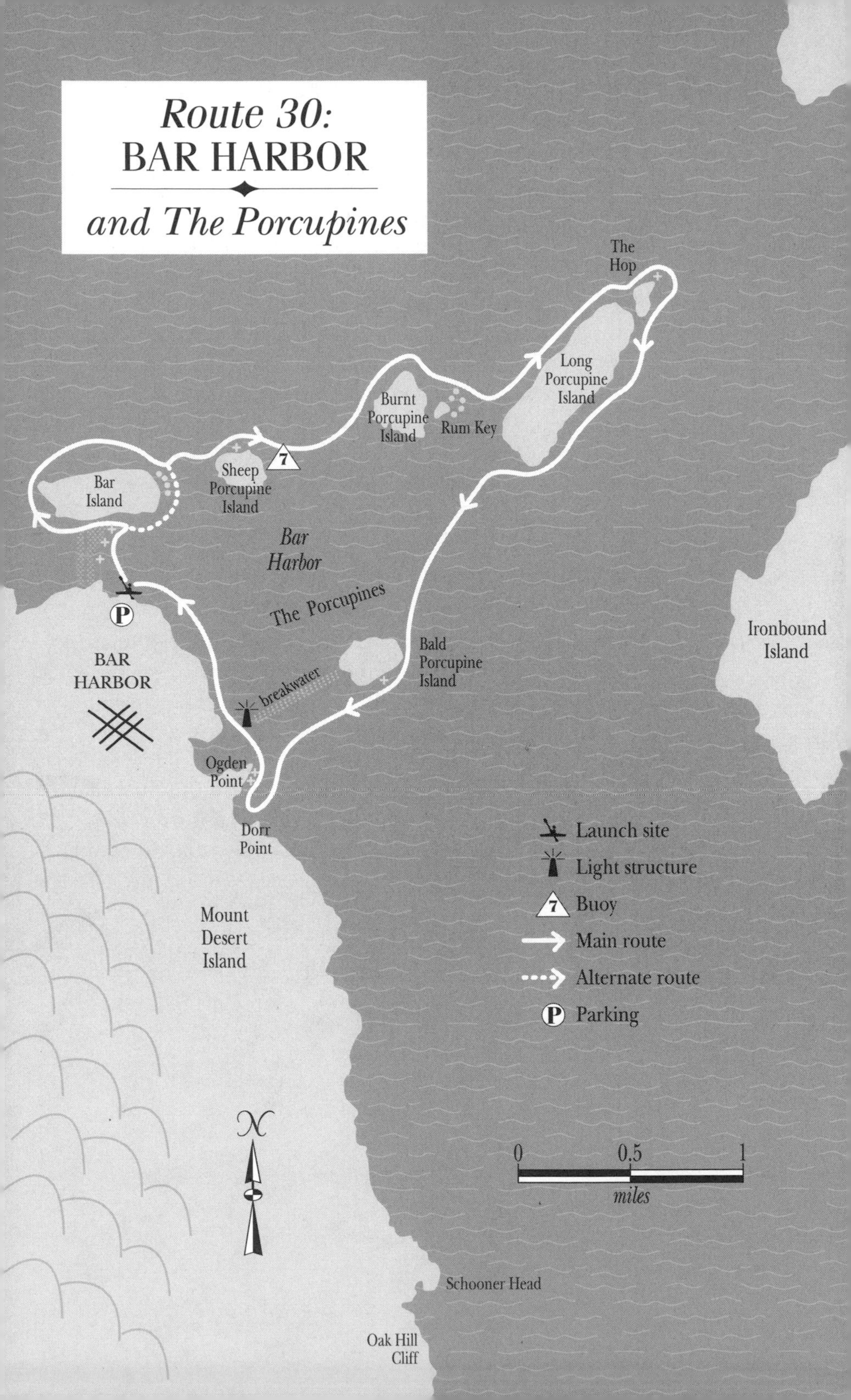

Route 30:
BAR HARBOR
◆
and The Porcupines

The Hop

Long Porcupine Island

Burnt Porcupine Island

Rum Key

Bar Island

Sheep Porcupine Island

7

Bar Harbor

The Porcupines

Bald Porcupine Island

Ironbound Island

BAR HARBOR

breakwater

Ogden Point

Dorr Point

Mount Desert Island

Launch site

Light structure

7 Buoy

→ Main route

···→ Alternate route

Ⓟ Parking

N

0   0.5   1
miles

Schooner Head

Oak Hill Cliff

CAUTIONS: Fog and boat traffic. Some open water with wind exposure, choppy conditions.

LAUNCH SITES: The Bar Harbor municipal ramp sits adjacent to a highly congested area where all the tour boats dock and there is a constant coming and going of vessels of many sizes. There is a small beach next to the ramp that is roomier for kayakers (until high tide) and won't block other boaters' access to the ramp. Parking is a problem at the municipal ramp. During the summer months there is a three-hour limit at the town lot, so you'll need to unload and then park elsewhere and hike back. A better choice is to park and launch from Albert Meadows, where you may leave your car for the day. Head up the hill on Main Street for 0.2 mile and turn left onto Albert Meadows Street. The parking area is at the end of this road. The launch is a short hand-carry to the water. This launch is best at high water under calm conditions. Low-tide launches are slippery but possible. If you don't like the looks of launching at Albert Meadows, just use it as your parking site and walk back to the town ramp.

LOCAL ATTRACTIONS: Acadia is the second most popular national park in the country and the most popular destination point in Maine. Plan on being overwhelmed with options—and crowds—during the summer months. Acadia National Park is a treasure with its restored carriage roads and spectacular scenery full of hiking trails, climbing spots, quiet ponds, mountain bike trails, campgrounds, and a wealth of wildlife. The town of Bar Harbor offers all the services even the most jaded tourist could demand.

Route 31

The Cranberries

The Cranberry Islands sit off the southern shore of Mount Desert Island absorbing the seas and wind from the open waters of the Gulf of Maine. They form an effective shield for the entrance to Somes Sound as it ventures into the heart of Mount Desert Island, as well as for the two harbors that sit to either side of its mouth, Southwest Harbor and Northeast Harbor. This group of islands includes Baker Island, an Acadia National Park holding; the privately owned enclaves of Bear Island and Sutton Island; and both Great and Little Cranberry Islands, with their year-round population.

Several launch sites will put you within range of the Cranberries and allow a visit to the town of Islesford on Little Cranberry Island, where you'll find a public dock and small landing beach. When you stand on the beach at Seal Harbor, the Cranberry Islands look surprisingly close, a paddle of just 2 miles or so to the ferry dock at Islesford. But this paddle can turn dicey in a hurry as afternoon winds develop or a fog bank moves into the area.

Exploring the outer edges of the Cranberry Islands requires great caution, especially around the shoals between Baker Island and Little Cranberry Island and along the southern shores of Great Cranberry and Baker Islands. The southerly exposure of these areas coupled with the topography of the bottom and the many ledges that dot the area should set off warning bells; proceed cautiously.

The launch site closest to the Cranberries is from the beach at Seal Harbor. This is a very nice launch site—except at low tide, when you have to lug your stuff a considerable distance to reach the water. But it's a treat to launch from the soft beach. No trailered boats can use this spot. There are all-tide boat ramps at Southwest Harbor, Manset, and Northeast Harbor, which can serve as launch sites for a paddle out to the Cranberries as well.

The Cranberries

As you paddle from Seal Harbor, you'll cross Eastern Way, a busy channel with a wide variety of boat traffic. Bear Island sits to the west near the entrance to Northeast Harbor, and large Sutton Island looms to your right across the channel. Depending on the wind direction and your planned paddling mileage, you can set a direct course for Cranberry Harbor or swing around Bear Island and its lighthouse (now leased to summer residents) and the western side of Sutton. This latter course gives you better protection from the east and minimizes the time you spend in the channel. Keep an eye out for both harbor seals and the larger and rarer gray seal as you paddle out to the Cranberries.

As you enter Cranberry Harbor, you'll see the ferry dock at Islesford on Little Cranberry Island to your left. You can land on either side of the town dock and explore the town of Islesford. There are rest rooms, a restaurant, and a small museum nearby. The walk into the village is pleasant and takes you past the church, schoolhouse, and cemetery. Before landing at Islesford, you might want to paddle across to the Pool which is tucked into the eastern side of Great Cranberry Island. This is an area of warm, shallow water that draws shorebirds, cormorants, and gulls. A glance at the chart will show you the large, inaccessible marsh on Great Cranberry from which the islands got their name.

If the winds are light and you have the paddling skills to venture into exposed and open waters, you can continue on to Baker Island, heading in either direction around Little Cranberry depending on the conditions. The shoals that extend from Bar Point can nearly close off the passage between Little Cranberry Island and Baker Island at low tide. The currents through here can be strong, and when opposed by the wind they are downright treacherous. Proceed with great caution. You may land in the pocket of shoreline on the northwest corner of Baker Island. A path leads to the lighthouse, which is centered on the high ground of the island. Most of Baker Island is owned by Acadia National Park and is open to day use.

As the day wears on, be aware of any strengthening of the wind or change in its direction. You must also keep a wary eye out for fog banks. These often move into the area during the summer months. And of course, don't forget to enjoy the spectacular views of the peaks on Mount Desert Island to the north and northwest.

TRIP HIGHLIGHTS: Island communities, lighthouses, and a challenging paddle to an offshore island group.

TRIP DURATION/LENGTH: This trip can range from 2.5 to 12 miles, depending on your propensity to explore and what conditions allow. If you are not comfortable with crossing to the outer islands, you may enjoy some fine shoreline paddling around Bear Island and Greening Island and plan stops at Southwest Harbor, Manset, or Northeast Harbor for a full day of exploring.

NAVIGATIONAL AIDS: Chart 13318 Frenchman Bay and Mount Desert Island (1:40,000). Can buoy at Seal Harbor; cans at entrance to Cranberry Harbor; Bowden Ledge buoy; Baker Island and Bear Island Lights; lighted bell buoys between Sutton Island and Northeast Harbor; nun buoy off Eastern Point (Greening Island).

CAUTIONS: Fog and possible deteriorating conditions during the crossing and over the course of the day. Boat traffic. Strong

The Cranberries

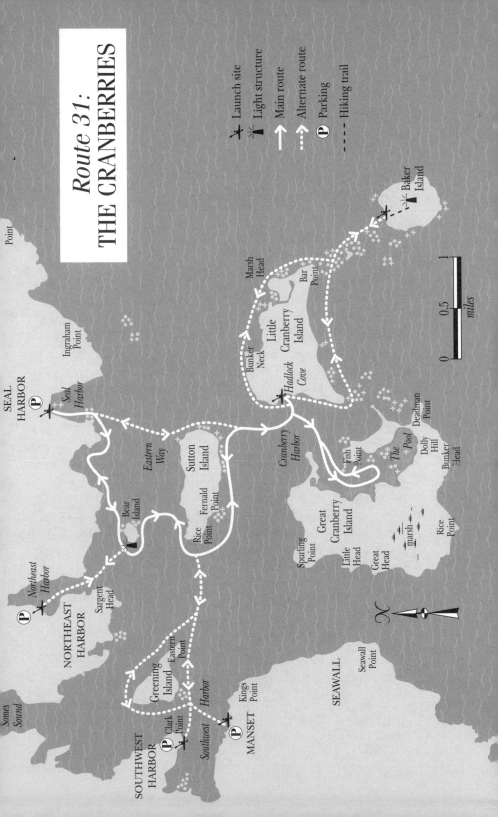

Route 31:
THE CRANBERRIES

Launch site
Light structure
Main route
Alternate route
Parking
Hiking trail

Somes Sound

Point

SEAL HARBOR

Ingraham Point

Seal Harbor

Eastern Way

Sutton Island

Fernald Point

Rice Point

Bear Island

Northeast Harbor

NORTHEAST HARBOR

Sargent Head

Greening Island

Eastern Point

SOUTHWEST HARBOR

Clark Point

Southwest Harbor

Kings Point

MANSET

SEAWALL

Seawall Point

Spurling Point

Little Head

Great Head

Great Cranberry Island

marsh

Rice Point

Bunker Head

Dolly Hill

Deadman Point

The Pool

Fish Point

Cranberry Harbor

Hadlock Cove

Bunker Neck

Little Cranberry Island

Bar Point

Marsh Head

Baker Island

miles

0   0.5   1

currents between Baker Island and Little Cranberry Island can be treacherous.

LAUNCH SITE: Seal Harbor sits about 3 miles east of Northeast Harbor on Route 3. There is a large beach alongside the road, where you'll see a sign for the turn to the Stanley Brook Entrance to Acadia National Park. It can get congested here on a hot, sunny day, so plan to arrive early. This site is open for day use only. You can see green can #1, which sits at the mouth of the harbor. Southwest Harbor has a large boat ramp that is very congested; parking is at a premium. Instead, try nearby Manset to the south, where there is a gravel ramp and a bit more parking. Take Route 102A toward Seawall Campground and turn onto Mansell Lane at the Double J Grocery (where they make good, hearty sandwiches). Follow this road to its end and turn left onto Shore Road. A short way down you will find the boat ramp and parking area on your right. Northeast Harbor provides an all-tide boat ramp and large parking area that extends across the road. This town launch sits to the east of Main Street and has rest room facilities and a friendly harbormaster's office. Like Southwest Harbor, this area is very congested. You'd do well to get an early start.

LOCAL ATTRACTIONS: Some of the most luxurious lodging accommodations on the island can be found in Northeast Harbor and Southwest Harbor. The Claremont Hotel (207–244–5036), Lindenwood Inn (207–244–5335), and Harbour Cottage Inn (207–244–5738) are found in Southwest Harbor; The Harbourside Inn (207–276–3272) and Maison Suisse Inn (207–276–5223) in Northeast Harbor. You can catch the mail boat out of Northeast Harbor for a run to the Cranberries or a National Park excursion to Baker Island. Both towns have bike rentals. There are numerous hiking trails throughout the area.

The Cranberries

Route 32

Seal Cove to Bartlett Narrows

This trip explores the western shores of Mount Desert Island, Bartlett Narrows, and Pretty Marsh Harbor. It is a very picturesque piece of paddling. Except for Bar Harbor, you'll probably see more sea kayaks plying these waters than anywhere on Mount Desert Island. The Bartlett Narrows boat ramp has become so popular that town officials have considered closing it to all but permit holders, and may well have done so by now. For this reason, we suggest launching at Seal Cove to the south. You can enjoy the same scenery and a wonderful lunch stop at the Pretty Marsh picnic area. With a bit more paddling, you can circle Bartlett Island and cruise the narrows to enjoy the seals, porpoises, and other wildlife species that abound in this area.

Two public-access islands sit off Bartlett Island: the Hub off the northern point and John Island, which sits at the southern end of Bartlett Narrows. The Hub should not be approached during the seal pupping season from May through mid-June. These ledges are active seal haul-outs, and great care should be taken around them whenever seals are present. John Island, sitting just outside Pretty Marsh Harbor, makes a nice lunch-stop alternative to Pretty Marsh picnic area. Please be careful not to contribute to any bank erosion as you explore this popular island.

As you depart Seal Cove, head north toward the private Moose and Hardwood Islands, the latter with fish pens off its eastern shore. You can continue on this course and paddle the western shore of Bartlett Island, approaching

Bartlett Narrows from the north. The tidal current runs through the Narrows at about 2 knots during the middle of the tide. You can also approach from the south if the tide is flooding, but remember to check the wind direction for the more exposed paddling section around the western side of Bartlett Island. Of course, you may prefer to cruise the narrows and explore into Western Bay instead of circling Bartlett Island before heading to your picnic stop at Pretty Marsh. There are many ways to plan this trip.

Acadia National Park owns the picnic site at Pretty

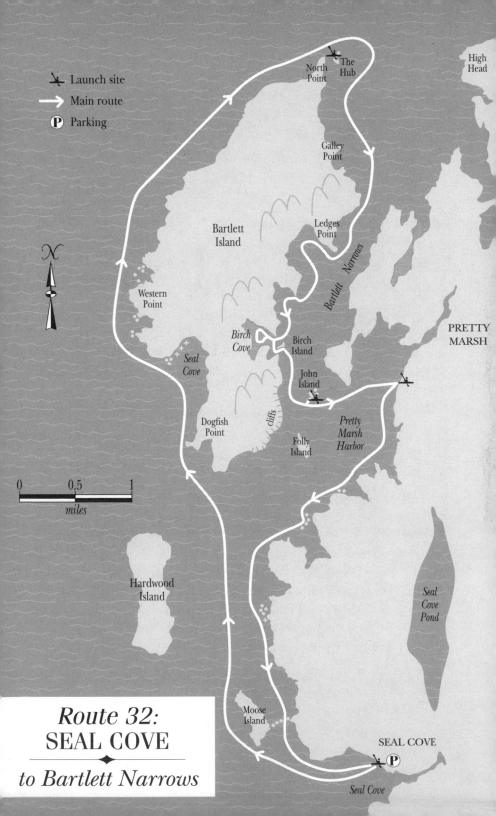

High
Head

North
Point

The
Hub

Galley
Point

Bartlett
Island

Ledges
Point

Bartlett Narrows

PRETTY
MARSH

Western
Point

*Birch
Cove*

Birch
Island

John
Island

*Pretty
Marsh
Harbor*

*Seal
Cove*

Dogfish
Point

cliffs

Folly
Island

Seal
Cove
Pond

Hardwood
Island

Moose
Island

SEAL COVE

Ⓟ

Seal Cove

Launch site

Main route

Ⓟ Parking

N

0   0.5   1
miles

Route 32:
SEAL COVE
◆
to Bartlett Narrows

Marsh Harbor. You'll see the set of steps and gazebo on the eastern shore just inside the harbor entrance. You can pull your boats up and access the picnic tables by climbing the steps. Pretty Marsh Harbor is a restful place with a tiny finger of water at its northeastern end that begs to be explored. If you prefer an island lunch stop, land on John Island off West Point.

TRIP HIGHLIGHTS: Harbor seals, ospreys, and one of the most scenic paddles in Maine.

TRIP DURATION/LENGTH: The round-trip paddle from Seal Cove around Bartlett Island with a stop at Pretty Marsh Harbor is about 15.5 miles. You may lop off the trip around Bartlett to save 5 miles of paddling if needed. You can always increase the mileage with forays into Western Bay to the north of Bartlett Narrows, or even explore to the south of Seal Cove if conditions permit.

NAVIGATIONAL AIDS: Chart 13316 Approaches to Blue Hill Bay (1:40,000).

CAUTIONS: Boat traffic and chop through the Narrows. Exposed conditions on the western side of Bartlett Island.

LAUNCH SITE: Seal Cove has a small cobble beach, all-tide boat ramp, grassy picnic knoll, and paved parking area. On Route 102 look for a SEAL COVE road sign that sits 0.3 mile before the left turn (as you approach from the south) onto Cape Road. If you miss this turn, a second Cape Road left turn will take you back around. Half a mile after you turn onto Cape Road, you will see the launch site and widened parking area.

LOCAL ATTRACTIONS: You have all the amenities and places to explore that Mount Desert Island and the National Park Service offer. Nearby Long Pond and Echo Pond to the east both make fine freshwater paddling trips and have convenient public boat ramps. Lodging in Manset and Bass Harbor is generally less expensive than in nearby Southwest Harbor. The Bass Harbor Inn (207–244–5157), The Moorings Inn (207–244–5523), and The Dockside (207–244–5221) all fit the bill nicely.

Seal Cove to Bartlett Narrows

Route 33

Sorrento to Sullivan

Sorrento sits at the southern point of Waukeag Neck at the head of Frenchman Bay. This entire area is absolutely beautiful for kayaking, but it demands good trip planning. A strong or sustained southerly blow should make you reconsider your plans for paddling in this area. We've sat in the parking lot at the boat ramp and watched the town floats buck and roll as lumpy conditions moved in from the south. Consider, too, the danger of a strong northerly offshore breeze.

As you explore this area, you need to be very careful about placing yourself into open, exposed areas. Frenchman Bay is renowned for its ability to turn rough very quickly and while the fetch is somewhat broken up by the islands off Bar Harbor, there's still a long stretch of water before waves spend their energy on the shores of Hancock Point and the southern shores of Dram and Preble Islands. The tidal flow through Sullivan Harbor as the bays empty from the north can stand on end when opposed by a strong wind from the south.

Yet if conditions are benign and you can work the tidal currents in your favor, this is a wonderful paddle with dramatic views of Mount Desert Island to the southwest. You can launch in Sorrento, paddle up into Sullivan Harbor, and—making sure you are working only within the upper half of the tide—access a small picnic area at Long Cove. This site sits alongside Route 1 but is surprisingly pleasant as you turn your back to the road and have a view across the calm waters of Long Cove. The climb up from the water is

not difficult, and there are picnic tables and pit toilets at this shady rest stop. Do not be tempted to push the tide or you will have a horrible slog back to deeper water, since Long Cove dries completely at low tide. From Long Cove you can continue to explore to the north as far as Sullivan Falls, where there is a swift run of water and a reversing falls that should be avoided. Even at slack water you should not be tempted to proceed through this area, because the return trip may well be turbulent and dangerous.

On one leg of your trip you should check out the two islands, Preble and Dram, which sit right at the entrance to Sorrento Harbor. These islands are owned and protected by The Nature Conservancy and open to careful day use year-round. Ospreys nest on these islands, so keep well away from any nesting sites. There are several cobble beaches for landing along the southern shore, but no interior trails on either of these undeveloped islands. The shoals off Preble Island separate Sorrento Harbor from Eastern Point Harbor at low tide and will prevent you from paddling the full length of the eastern shore of Preble Island unless you are willing to sneak through by pulling your kayak over the slippery rocks that block the way.

Flanders Bay to the east makes for some fine exploring but there is no public access once you pass Preble Island. If you don't have a cooperative tide for the paddle to the Sullivan picnic site, the paddle into Flanders Bay makes a

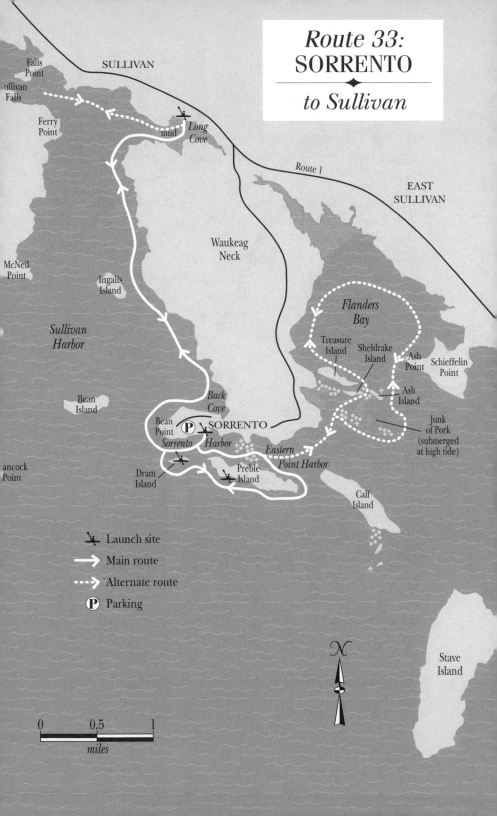

SULLIVAN

Falls
Point

Sullivan
Falls

Ferry
Point

mud

Long
Cove

Route 1

EAST
SULLIVAN

McNeil
Point

Ingalls
Island

Waukeag
Neck

Flanders
Bay

Treasure
Island

Sheldrake
Island

Ash
Point

Schieffelin
Point

Ash
Island

Sullivan
Harbor

Bean
Island

Back
Cove

Bean
Point

SORRENTO

Junk
of Pork
(submerged
at high tide)

Sorrento
Harbor

Hancock
Point

Dram
Island

Preble
Island

Eastern
Point Harbor

Calf
Island

Launch site

Main route

Alternate route

P Parking

N

Stave
Island

0   0.5   1
miles

nice alternative and is well protected. The area around Sheldrake Island, Junk of Pork, and Ash Island is interesting; when uncovered at low tide, it creates an extensive gravel bar where cormorants and gulls abound. You can build in a leisurely stop on Preble Island or Dram Island for a shoreline leg stretch or picnic lunch if needed.

TRIP HIGHLIGHTS: Incredible views of the mountains of Mount Desert and the sweep of Frenchman Bay.

TRIP DURATION/LENGTH: The round trip from Sorrento to Long Cove is about 7 miles. Unless conditions prevent it, you'll want to add some paddling around Dram and Preble Islands, so the full trip clocks in at closer to 10 miles. The Flanders Bay alternative can range from 6 to 10 miles.

NAVIGATIONAL AIDS: Chart 13318 Frenchman Bay and Mount Desert Island (1:40,000). Nun buoy west of Dram Island; channel can off Long Cove; Halftide Ledge buoy.

CAUTIONS: Wind exposure and seas from the south. Choppy conditions are common and can turn challenging as the wind opposes the tidal current. Mudflats at Long Cove.

LAUNCH SITE: Sorrento Harbor has an all-tide, concrete boat ramp and a nice gravel beach for launching kayaks to the right of the parking area. There is limited parking, so on summer weekends the lot will likely be full by midmorning. There is a portable toilet behind the fence next to the parking lot. To reach the ramp, follow Route 185 south from Route 1 on either West Shore Road or East Side Road—they both end up in the same spot. Once they rejoin, go 0.7 mile and bear left onto Kearsarge Avenue. Follow this 0.1 mile to the town dock and ramp.

LOCAL ATTRACTIONS: Sorrento is a small town with lots of summer rentals and seasonal homes. Nearby Ellsworth provides shopping and amenities. There are a few small stops for gas and groceries along Route 1 before you reach the hustle and bustle of Ellsworth. There are also numerous motels and inns in Ellsworth, especially along Route 3 just outside of town. In town, you'll find some fun shopping at The Grasshopper Shop, and you can stuff yourself at The Mex after a day of paddling.

Clothing as Gear

Adequate clothing for protection from Maine's chilly waters is a must for sea kayakers. Only the foolhardy would set out in the early part of paddling season without the protection of a wetsuit or drysuit. Water temperatures usually begin to creep above the midfifties by early June or later, so any outing must consider the potential for immersion and the temperature of the water.

Wetsuits work by trapping a thin layer of water next to your skin, which is rapidly warmed by your body heat then insulated by the suit's neoprene. Most paddling wetsuits are 3 millimeters thick, slightly less than a typical scuba diver's wetsuit. A drysuit is made of waterproof material that is closed at the neck, ankles, and wrists by latex gaskets. Inside the drysuit you will remain dry, but you'll need some warm layers next to your body.

Cotton clothing is not an appropriate choice for Maine's waters. Cotton will rapidly cool you when it gets wet; it also becomes heavy, since it can absorb so much water. Stick with quick-drying materials and fabrics, which continue to provide warmth even when wet. Consider windproof materials for your outer layers, even when wearing a wetsuit.

It is always tempting to ignore the need for clothing to protect you from cold water temperatures on sunny, warm days. If you are worried about overheating, remember how much cold water you're surrounded by; a dampened hat or bandanna will cool you down if needed. You'll also have the perfect excuse for a water fight!

Downeast: Milbridge *to* Machias

Route 34

Pleasant River

The Pleasant River is just that: a pleasant stretch of water that is rich in wildlife. The salt marshes along the upper stretches of the river are home to an incredible variety of shorebirds and wading birds: plovers, yellowlegs, and sandpipers can been seen along the banks on either side of high tide; great blue herons and snowy egrets stalk the area throughout the paddling season. At low tide you will be hemmed in by the rich mudflats and the marsh grasses, which are brilliant green in the early summer. The river widens below Bray Point and its cluster of navigational buoys, and begins to feel more coastal as you approach the upper reaches of Pleasant Bay and the islands at the mouth of the river.

There are several large, interesting coves along the western shore that deserve exploring when there is sufficient water. In particular, Upper Wass Cove and Lower Wass Cove are worth a look, with their slivers of water that slice into the land. As you pass by the rolling farmland at Whites Point, you may see llamas grazing alongside the Pleasant Bay Bed and Breakfast on the hill. It can be rather startling to be bird-watching and have one of these animals appear through your binoculars! On the northern side of Wass Point, there is a small spit of gravel that makes a nice rest stop and leg stretch. Locals will often launch boats here, but you're best off using this spot only for a break and not as a boat launch since this is not public property.

Carrying Place Cove is a beautiful and protected tuck-in on Ripley Neck that for early travelers made for an easy portage to the waters of the Harrington River and saved the more exposed and longer trip around the end of Ripley Neck. Raspberry Island, Mink Island, and the Birch Islands make a fine sight sitting in the channel just below Carrying Place Cove. You should give an especially wide berth to Upper Birch Island until deep into August; there is an important great blue heron rookery here, which is protected by The Nature Conservancy. Don't land on any of these islands.

You can continue your trip to include a paddle around the cluster of islands that sit off the southern end of Ripley Neck or begin the return leg to Addison at any point. A strong southerly may create some sizable breaks on the ledges in this area; be cautious as you pick your way through these waters.

You may choose to spot a vehicle at both Addison and at the Milbridge town ramp on the Narraguagus River for a point-to-point trip in either direction, depending on the conditions. Do not count on any of the other boat launches noted in the *Maine Atlas and Gazetteer* for this area. You will waste valuable time trying to determine their location, and the residential development that has begun along these shores makes public access a long shot at best. The point-to-point trip is considerably more exposed as you head out into Narraguagus Bay and should not be undertaken in windy conditions or following a sustained southerly wind or storms to the south that could create large swells. The Narraguagus River below the Milbridge ramp is a narrow, dredged channel that should be run with the tide unless you like a good workout. The tidal current is stronger here than on the Pleasant River, so you'll need good planning and lucky timing to work it all to your advantage.

TRIP HIGHLIGHTS: Rolling farmland, salt-water marshes and mudflats teeming with bird life. Quiet coves and unspoiled coastline.

TRIP DURATION/LENGTH: Obviously, you can cover as little or as much distance as you wish on the round trip from the Addison boat ramp. A paddle the length of the river, around the islands off the southern end of Ripley Neck, and back to Addison is just less than 14 miles. The leg stretch at Wass Point is about 3 miles south of Addison; it is 5 miles to Carrying Place Cove. If you plan this as a point-to-point trip from Milbridge to Addison (or the reverse), you will paddle about 11 miles taking the route between Dyer Island and Foster Island.

NAVIGATIONAL AIDS: Chart 13324 Tibbett Narrows to Schoodic Island (1:40,000). Buoys off Bray Point; Bunker Ledge and Strout Island Ledges buoys; can buoys in Dyer Island narrows; channel buoys in Narraguagus River.

CAUTIONS: Mudflats and a steady tidal current on the Pleasant River. Considerable exposure during the middle third of the trip between Milbridge and Addison. Ledge breaks at Ripley Neck.

LAUNCH SITE: The turn off Route 1 for the town of Addison is best taken at the well-marked intersection with Main Street in Columbia Falls. This is a very sharp right if you're traveling from

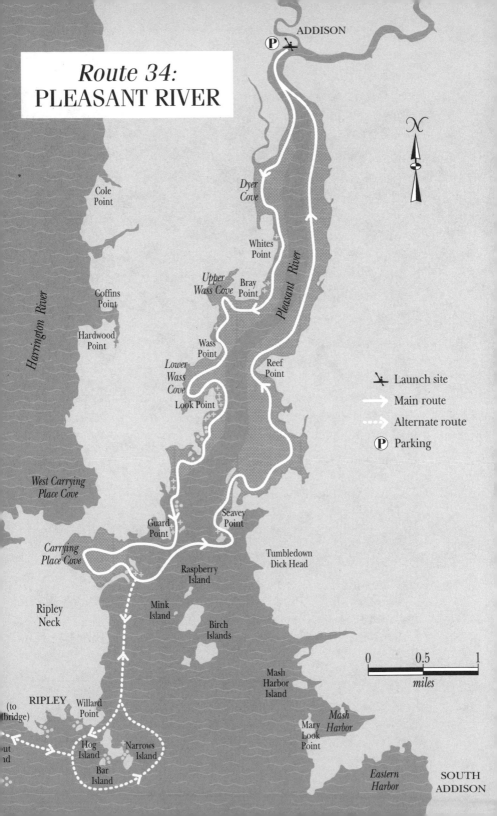

Route 34:
PLEASANT RIVER

ADDISON

Dyer
Cove

Whites
Point

*Upper
Wass Cove*   Bray
Point

Cole
Point

Coffins
Point

Hardwood
Point

Harrington River

Wass
Point

*Lower
Wass
Cove*

Look Point

Pleasant River

Reef
Point

Launch site

Main route

Alternate route

P Parking

*West Carrying
Place Cove*

Guard
Point

Seavey
Point

*Carrying
Place Cove*

Tumbledown
Dick Head

Raspberry
Island

Ripley
Neck

Mink
Island

Birch
Islands

Mash
Harbor
Island

RIPLEY

Willard
Point

(to
bridge)

ut
d

Hog
Island

Narrows
Island

Bar
Island

Mary
Look
Point

*Mash
Harbor*

*Eastern
Harbor*

SOUTH
ADDISON

0   0.5   1
miles

N

the south, but it's easier to spot than the earlier turnoff outside Harrington. Follow Addison Road and then Point Street to Water Street. Go past the post office and look for the ramp on your left. This is an all-tide concrete ramp; there is a gravel parking lot above it. The Milbridge boat ramp can be seen from Route 1A as you cross the bridge over the Narraguagus River. Take the first right-hand turn after the bridge and follow this around to the ramp and large parking area on your right.

LOCAL ATTRACTIONS: The town of Milbridge offers the most in terms of groceries, a deli, and lodging options. The Pleasant Bay Bed and Breakfast (207–483–4490) at Whites Point on the western shore of the Pleasant River is kayak friendly, and you can check out those llamas.

Route 35

Crowley Island

Crowley Island is a large inhabited island just west of Jonesport. Bounded on the west by the West River and on the east by the Indian River, it can offer hours of protected paddling and even a circumnavigation if the tide is just right. At the head of Crowley Island, you cross under a newly constructed wooden bridge that poses no problem for kayakers. There is no way to cross from the Indian River to the West (or vice versa) except at half tide or better. Large areas drain to expose mudflats and there isn't enough water to proceed, even for kayakers. There are many options for making this trip work with tides in your favor, though, since you have the option of proceeding up either side of the island. There is a nice little rest stop on Indian River Island (not marked on the chart), which sits at the mouth of the cove leading into the village of Indian River. This tiny, wooded island is accessible only at half tide or better; keep an eye on your watch and the water so you don't get stranded on an ebbing tide. While circumnavigating Crowley Island requires some planning and a keen eye on your watch, it is well worth the effort. The trip is relaxing (except for keeping time) and generally quite placid. It is particularly beautiful in the fall, because a good mix of hardwoods and conifers lines the shores.

Even if your schedule and the tide tables don't cooperate, you can explore the southern end of Crowley and the islands and ledges that dot this area. You also have the option of proceeding west to Daniels Island, which sits just off Bare Point. Daniels is accessible only during the top two-thirds of the tide, though you may be able to push this a bit if you approach from the south. This side trip to Daniels does expose you to strong southerly winds for a bit, but there's cover to duck behind for most of the way.

TRIP HIGHLIGHTS: Wooded, undeveloped shoreline. A serene and quiet trip along two stretches of tidal river.

TRIP/DURATION LENGTH: The circumnavigation requires a bit more than 9 miles of paddling. Exploring along the southern end of Crowley and paddling out to Daniels Island makes for 8 miles or more, depending on your propensity for poking around.

NAVIGATIONAL AIDS: Chart 13326 Machias Bay to Tibbett Narrows (1:40,000). Moosebec Reach buoys.

CAUTIONS: An ebb tide that cannot be ignored around Crowley Island. Moosebec Reach boat traffic and the current beneath the Beals Island bridge. Exposed conditions on the approach to Daniels Island.

LAUNCH SITE: It is best to use the Jonesport public boat ramp on Sawyer Square Road for this trip, since you will not have to cross Moosebec Reach. As you travel along the main road through town (Route 187, a clearly marked turnoff from Route 1), look for the CITGO sign, Homeport Diner, and T.A. King and Sons Trustworthy Hardware. Turn onto Sawyer Square Road and head toward the water, looking for the blue BOAT RAMP sign. You can also launch

Crowley Island

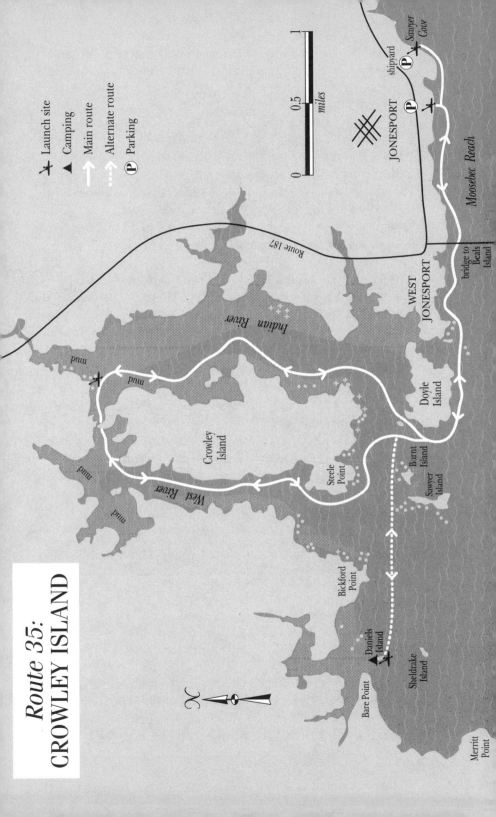

Route 35:
CROWLEY ISLAND

from the Jonesport Shipyard just north of town (207–497–2701). There is protected parking and a nice boat ramp (usable at all but the lowest low tides) for a fee of $5.00 per kayak and $1.00 per night parking.

Note: Launching from the mainland puts you into Moosebec Reach, where there is a great deal of boat traffic and some current that ebbs to the west and floods to the east. If you have to travel against the tide, paddle along the fringe of the channel and use the eddies. Avoid the middle of the tide. If you're opposing it, you're in for some hard work. The current under the Beals Island bridge is even stronger because of the constriction caused by the bridgeworks; it may create strong eddy lines. Again, avoid this area during the middle of the tide.

If you want to check out the head of Crowley Island in advance, look for a sign to Crowley Island just before you cross a very narrow section of the Indian River off Route 187 and the village of Indian River. This dirt road has a spot to pull over just before the bridge so you can get out and reconnoiter.

LOCAL ATTRACTIONS: Jonesport is home to a renowned lobster fishing fleet and celebrates lobster boat races on July Fourth (you do *not* want to be kayaking in Moosebec Reach on that day). There are several small bed-and-breakfasts in town: Tootsie's Bed-and-Breakfast (207–497–5414), Harbor House on Sawyer Cove (207–497–5417), or the kayak-friendly Raspberry Shores (207–497–2463). You should also consider driving farther north to Machias, where you'll find several small motels like the Machias Motor Inn (207–255–4861) and Helen's Restaurant (207–255–8423). Helen's is famous for good meals and homemade pies (strawberry has achieved local cult status). There is also a public boat ramp adjacent to Helen's where you can launch for a quick paddle to burn off calories and make room for a second piece of pie.

If the weather is too foggy or windy for paddling, consider driving to the trailhead of the Great Wass Island Preserve and explore this area on foot. The trails traverse a fascinating variety of landscapes and are well worth the trip (even adding an extra day in the area). To reach the trails, drive onto Great Wass Island and bear right onto Black Duck Cove Road. This will turn to dirt. Continue for about 3 miles until you see a small parking area on your left with a sign for The Nature Conservancy.

Route 36

The Sands

This is an adventurous trip to a wild and lovely spot of land that is only barely exposed at high tide. In fact, this slip of land may be awash during storm surges and spring high tides. The views from its shores are spectacular as you look across Western Bay toward Great Wass or west to Cape Split and the islands outside Tibbetts Narrows. This small island, more sandbar and exposed ledge than anything else, sits just 100 yards or so south of Inner Sands, which is marked on the chart. Neither Inner nor Outer Sands Island is accessible to the public. This entire area is rich in wildlife, so please move quietly and avoid disturbing any nest sites or seal haul-out areas that you might observe.

This is particularly true in the late spring and early summer—nesting and seal pupping season. For this reason, we suggest making this trip in the fall. You'll make less impact, and the days are more likely to be clear and the visibility excellent.

It is best to launch from Jonesport and proceed along the northern side of Moosebec Reach to explore the Goose Islands before paddling south towards Shabbit and Duck Ledges. You can continue down the string of islands—which includes Stevens, Little Drisko, and Drisko—for protection along the way and great exploring along these shores. While you do have some protection from southwesterly winds as you pick your way among the islands, this trip should not be undertaken in a strong offshore breeze (north to northwest). The stakes are too high if you must do battle against a strong wind that wants to push you into exposed waters with no bailout points available. Save this trip for calmer conditions and good visibility.

TRIP HIGHLIGHTS: A wild and remote paddle. Scrappy islands and the impressive western shore of Great Wass Island.

TRIP DURATION/LENGTH: This is a full day involving 14 or more miles of paddling to reach the Sands and return to Jonesport. Obviously, you can cut this trip short at any point before reaching the Sands, though there is no public access on any other islands along the way.

NAVIGATIONAL AIDS: Chart 13326 Machias Bay to Tibbett Narrows (1:40,000). Moosebec Reach buoys; lighted bell buoy at Fessenden Ledge; day beacons off Pom Island.

CAUTIONS: Offshore winds. Very exposed conditions. Fog. Current and boat traffic in Moosebec Reach.

LAUNCH SITE: It is best to use the Jonesport public boat ramp which leaves you with the shortest mileage. As you travel along the main road through town (Route 187, a clearly marked turnoff from Route 1), look for the CITGO sign, Homeport Diner, and

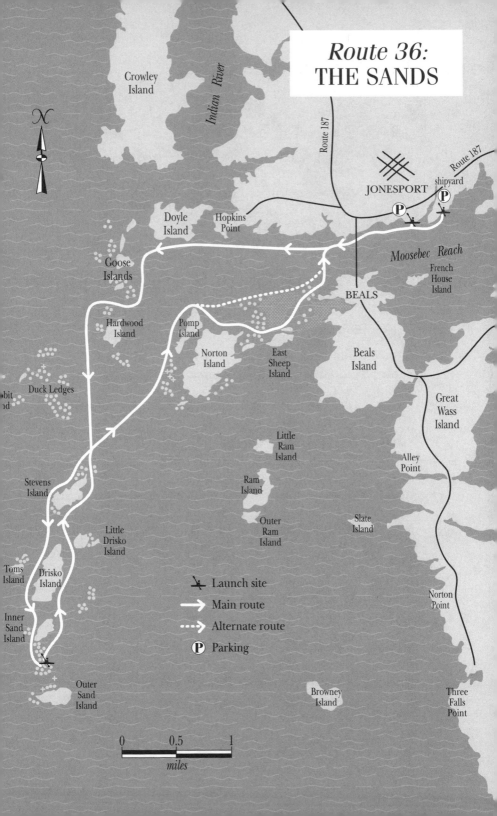

Route 36:
THE SANDS

Crowley
Island

Indian River

Route 187

Route 187

JONESPORT

shipyard
℗

℗

Moosebec Reach

Doyle
Island

Hopkins
Point

French
House
Island

Goose
Islands

BEALS

Hardwood
Island

Pomp
Island

Norton
Island

East
Sheep
Island

Beals
Island

Duck Ledges

Great
Wass
Island

bit
d

Little
Ram
Island

Alley
Point

Stevens
Island

Ram
Island

Little
Drisko
Island

Outer
Ram
Island

Slate
Island

Toms
Island

Driско
Island

Launch site

Norton
Point

Inner
Sand
Island

Main route

Alternate route

℗ Parking

Outer
Sand
Island

Browney
Island

Three
Falls
Point

0   0.5   1
miles

T.A. King and Sons Trustworthy Hardware. Turn onto Sawyer
Square Road and head toward the water, looking for the blue BOAT
RAMP sign. You can also launch from the Jonesport Shipyard just
north of town (207–497–2701). There is protected parking and a
nice boat ramp (usable at all but the lowest low tides) for a fee of
$5.00 per kayak and $1.00 per night parking.

   Note: Launching from the mainland puts you into Moosebec
Reach, where there is a great deal of boat traffic and some current
that ebbs to the west and floods to the east. If you have to travel
against the tide, paddle along the fringe of the channel and use
the eddies. Avoid the middle of the tide. If you're opposing it,
you're in for some hard work. The current under the Beals Island
bridge is even stronger because of the constriction caused by the
bridgeworks; it may create strong eddy lines. Again, avoid this area
during the middle of the tide.

LOCAL ATTRACTIONS: See Route 35: Crowley Island for
information on restaurants, lodging, and local attractions.

Route 37

————————————————————➤

Great Wass Eastern Shore

More than fifty islands make up the Great Wass Archipelago that sits off the Jonesport Peninsula. Many of these islands host the southern extreme of some species' ranges, providing invaluable nesting sites for seabirds and bald eagles, along with just the right mix of weather to nurture rare flora. The feeling of wildness here is palpable. The waters of the Bay of Fundy and the Gulf of Maine meet here to create a salty, damp environment of island peat bogs, stunted jack pines, and carnivorous plants. These islands are not meant for casual exploration. Instead, you sit quietly and absorb them.

The Nature Conservancy owns and manages many of the islands and island easements in this area. Many sites are closed entirely during the nesting season, February 15 through August 15. Bald eagles often begin nesting behaviors in February, and blue herons may still be on the nest in mid-August, so human interference must be kept to a minimum during these critical times. Other islands contain rare bog plants hanging on to fragile island soils that are easily damaged by foot traffic. It is important to adhere to any restrictions when visiting these areas.

Great Wass Island, the largest island in the archipelago, is home to more than 1,500 acres of protected land. Two hiking trails join along the shoreline on the eastern side of the island. The southern end of Great Wass at Red Head is a spectacular but exposed coastline that is likely to be encased in dense fog during much of the paddling season. Several large coves offer protection along the lower eastern side, as

does Mud Hole, a shallow slit of water that reaches well into the island near its midpoint.

Exploring the shores of Great Wass is rewarding, but you must be wary of approaching fog and—once you're in the fog—of other boat traffic. Kayakers are not common in these waters, so other boaters are less accustomed to our presence than they are around Mount Desert Island or Penobscot Bay. Avoid rounding the southern end of Great

Wass unless you have advanced paddling skills and are comfortable in large swells and the rebounding waves that are thrown from Red Head. In a strong offshore breeze, you are courting great danger. Instead, consider hiking the shoreline to Red Head after landing under protection to the north.

Several day trips originate from Great Wass or the town of Jonesport. All may well require the ability to navigate in dense fog. If you are unsure of your ability to do this, you should only consider a trip that hugs the shoreline of Great Wass, or the Crowley Island trip originating in Jonesport (see Route 35).

The easiest place to begin your explorations of the eastern shore of Great Wass Island is from the launch site on its northern end, just off Pig Island Gut. As you head east through the narrow gut, be careful to stay to the side. There is very little room for larger boats to maneuver here; many lobster boats charge through even in low-visibility conditions. They're making their daily runs to and from work, and keeping an eye out for kayakers is not a high priority. As you exit Pig Island Gut, beware the shoal areas with seaweed-covered ledges. Even kayakers may fetch up on these if they are not careful.

You can continue to follow the eastern shoreline of Great Wass for several hours or a full day, depending on the conditions and your preferences. The shoreline is varied and interesting and gets wilder below Mud Hole as you paddle by Nature Conservancy lands. You can duck into Mud Hole for a break from the wind if needed. Along the eastern shore you may land on Nature Conservancy property and access hiking trails at Mud Hole Point and Cape Cove. The landing is easier (except in a strong southerly wind) at Cape Cove, south of Little Cape Point, and the trail is marked by a cairn and a red mark on the rock. Make sure to pull kayaks well up into a protected area if you are planning to hike for any length of time. Hiking along the shoreline can be slippery, so move carefully. Please stay along the shoreline or on the marked trails as you explore on foot. These areas are open to the public for day use year-round.

You can continue to explore farther south down into Popplestone Cove, if you like, and may pull your boats into pockets for a hike along the shoreline or a picnic. Beyond Popplestone Cove please heed our earlier warnings about the southern end of Great Wass.

TRIP HIGHLIGHTS: Exploring the shoreline of one of the most impressive islands (and nature preserve) on the coast of Maine.

TRIP DURATION/LENGTH: This trip covers 8 or more miles, with shorter bailouts along the way if needed. There are plenty of side trips and small coves to explore for additional mileage. Mud Hole Point is about 2.7 miles from the launch site, and Popplestone Cove is about 5 miles.

NAVIGATIONAL AIDS: Chart 13326 Machias Bay to Tibbett Narrows (1:40,000). Pig Island Gut buoys.

CAUTIONS: Offshore winds. Fog and more fog. Very exposed conditions as you near Red Head. Boat traffic in Pig Island Gut.

LAUNCH SITE: The easiest site to launch from is the one on Great Wass Island next to Island Variety (207–497–2289). From Jonesport cross the Beals Island bridge, then cross the causeway to Great Wass. Bear left and follow the road to Island Variety. There are a couple of parking spots just beyond and across from the store and the launch site. The folks at Island Variety are willing to let you park in their lot for a small fee if there's room. There is very limited parking at this launch site. You may be forced to launch from the mainland in Jonesport, where there are two launch sites. One is the Jonesport public boat ramp on Sawyer Square Road. As you travel along the main road through town (Route 187, a clearly marked turnoff from Route 1), look for the CITGO sign, Homeport Diner, and T.A. King and Sons Trustworthy Hardware. Turn onto Sawyer Square Road and head toward the water, looking for the blue BOAT RAMP sign. You can also launch from the Jonesport

Route 187

JONESPORT

P **P**

Launch site

Light structure

Main route

Alternate route

P Parking

Hiking trail

Moosebec *Reach*

BEALS

Pig
Island

Beals
Island

Great
Wass
Island

Head Harbor
Island

Spectacle
Islands

Middle
Hardwood
Island

Crow
Point

*The Cows
Yard*

*Head
Harbor*

Hall
Island

Steele
Harbor
Island

Man
Island

*Mud
Hole*

Mud Hole
Point

Green
Island

Norton
Point

Little
Cape Point

Knight
Island

Mistake
Island

Great
Wass
Island

*Cape
Cove*

*Popplestone
Cove*

Little
Pond
Head

*The
Pond*

Red Head

Pond
Point

0   0.5   1
miles

Route 37:
GREAT WASS
EASTERN SHORE

Shipyard just north of town (207–497–2701). There is protected parking and a nice boat ramp (usable at all but the lowest low tides) for a fee of $5.00 per kayak and $1.00 per night parking.

Note: Launching from the mainland puts you into Moosebec Reach, where there is a great deal of boat traffic and some current that ebbs to the west and floods to the east. If you have to travel against the tide, paddle along the fringe of the channel and use the eddies. Avoid the middle of the tide. If you're opposing it, you're in for some hard work. The current under the Beals Island bridge is even stronger because of the constriction caused by the bridgeworks; it may create strong eddy lines. Again, avoid this area during the middle of the tide.

LOCAL ATTRACTIONS: See Route 35: Crowley Island for information on restaurants, lodging, and local attractions.

Route 38

Great Wass to Mistake Island

This is a beautiful and varied day of paddling, but it should be undertaken only under good visibility. If the fog clamps down on you, it is best to hug the nearest known shoreline and pick your way back along the eastern side of Eastern Bay; then shoot across to the south of Sheep Island, following the buoys into Pig Island Gut. While this is less direct, it will keep you out of boating channels as vessels head in through Main Channel Way and Mud Hole Channel. If you are fortunate enough to still be along the eastern shore of Great Wass when the fog moves in, you can simply backtrack along your route. If you don't believe that

fog can be a factor in this area, simply review the data from the Moose Peak Light, which is automated and operates in heavy fog an average of 1,600 hours a year. And of course, fog is most prevalent during the peak paddling months of July and August. Only the light at Petit Manan does more fog duty.

As you paddle across Eastern Bay, it is fairly easy to find bits of protection from a typical south or southwesterly wind. You can dart from Spectacle Island to Middle Hardwood Island to Little Hardwood Island. And there's plenty of protection in the coves along Head Harbor Island and Steele Harbor Island. Beware the lower third of the tide, because Middle Hardwood Island bars to Head Harbor Island. You can proceed along the western shore of Steele Harbor Island and cross the Main Channel Way to paddle between Knight and Mistake Islands. As you come along Knight Island, you will be treated to an impressive view of the Moose Peak Light that sits on Mistake Island. There is a decent place to pull up onto the rocks of Knight Island about halfway down the narrow channel between Knight and Mistake. While there are no nesting sites on Knight, please walk only on the rocks and avoid the vegetation on the northwestern end.

On the northwest end of Mistake Island, there is a small dock and access to a boardwalk that leads to the lighthouse. The boardwalk protects the fragile plants found here, and is provided by The Nature Conservancy in cooperation with the U.S. Coast Guard. The view into the Gulf of Maine is impressive and can make you feel pretty inconsequential. There is typically a sizable swell, which has built over the long fetch. You get a better idea of the size of the swells when you can observe a large fishing vessel plow through these waters; now imagine it in a kayak! If you look over to Man Island and Black Head to the northeast, you will probably see spray being thrown from the waves crashing on these shores.

Great Wass to Mistake Island

The ledges alongside Water Island, to the southwest, are popular seal haul-out spots and should be avoided, especially during the late-spring and early-summer months when pups are present. You can sit on Mistake Island and watch the activity through binoculars for hours of entertainment without disturbing them. While exploring this area, consider paddling up into the Cows Yard and Head Harbor for another spectacular view out into the Gulf of Maine. It is much safer to approach these areas through the entrance along Crow Point, rather than along the turbulent outer shore of Steele Harbor Island.

TRIP HIGHLIGHTS: Drop dead gorgeous scenery. Wild, remote islands full of bird life and unique flora. Moose Peak Light.

Great Wass to Mistake Island -205-

TRIP DURATION/LENGTH: Paddling to Mistake Island and back covers about 9 miles. There are lots of options for additional mileage as you explore the coves along Head Harbor and Steele Harbor Islands and check out the Cows Yard.

NAVIGATIONAL AIDS: Chart 13326 Machias Bay to Tibbett Narrows (1:40,000). Pig Island Gut buoys; can buoy off Spectacle Island; Moose Peak Light; can buoy off Calf Island.

CAUTIONS: Fog and more fog. Boat traffic in Pig Island Gut. Very exposed conditions on the outside of Mistake Island.

LAUNCH SITE: The easiest site to launch from is the one on Great Wass Island next to Island Variety (207–497–2289). From Jonesport cross the Beals Island bridge, then cross the causeway to Great Wass. Bear left and follow the road to Island Variety. There are a couple of parking spots just beyond and across from the store and the launch site. The folks at Island Variety are willing to let you park in their lot for a small fee if there's room. There is very limited parking at this launch site. You may be forced to launch from the mainland in Jonesport, where there are two launch sites. One is the Jonesport public boat ramp on Sawyer Square Road. As you travel along the main road through town (Route 187, a clearly marked turnoff from Route 1), look for the CITGO sign, Homeport Diner, and T.A. King and Sons Trustworthy Hardware. Turn onto Sawyer Square Road and head toward the water, looking for the blue BOAT RAMP sign. You can also launch from the Jonesport Shipyard just north of town (207–497–2701). There is protected parking and a nice boat ramp (usable at all but the lowest low tides) for a fee of $5.00 per kayak and $1.00 per night parking.

Note: Launching from the mainland puts you into Moosebec Reach, where there is a great deal of boat traffic and some current that ebbs to the west and floods to the east. If you have to travel against the tide, paddle along the fringe of the channel and use the eddies. Avoid the middle of the tide. If you're opposing it, you're in for some hard work. The current under the Beals Island bridge is even stronger because of the constriction caused by the bridgeworks; it may create strong eddy lines. Again, avoid this area during the middle of the tide.

LOCAL ATTRACTIONS: See Route 35: Crowley Island for information on restaurants, lodging, and local attractions.

Great Wass to Mistake Island

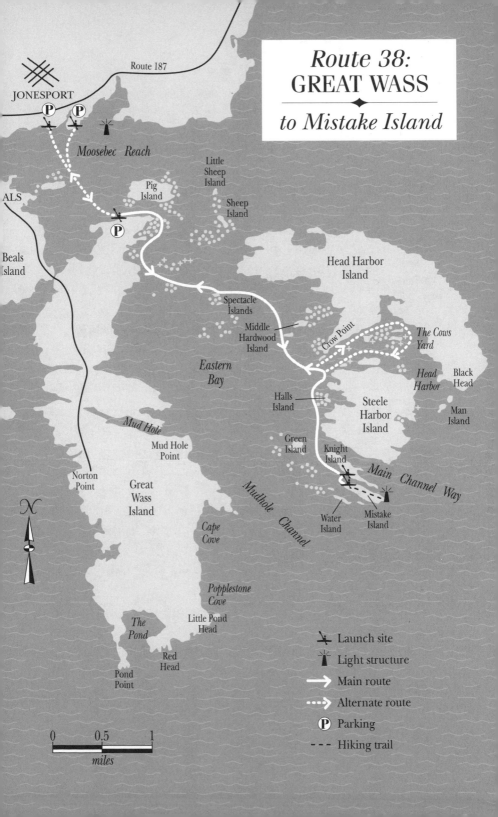

JONESPORT

Route 187

Moosebec Reach

ALS

Beals Island

Pig Island

Little Sheep Island

Sheep Island

Route 38:
GREAT WASS

to Mistake Island

Head Harbor Island

Spectacle Islands

Crow Point

The Cows Yard

Middle Hardwood Island

Head Harbor

Black Head

Man Island

Eastern Bay

Steele Harbor Island

Halls Island

Mud Hole

Mud Hole Point

Green Island

Knight Island

Main Channel Way

Norton Point

Mudhole Channel

Great Wass Island

Water Island

Mistake Island

N

Cape Cove

Popplestone Cove

Little Pond Head

The Pond

Red Head

Pond Point

Launch site

Light structure

Main route

Alternate route

Ⓟ Parking

Hiking trail

0   0.5   1
miles

Route 39

Roque Island Archipelago

he Roque Island Archipelago has long been considered one of the most beautiful areas to explore on the Maine coast. Cruising guides wax poetic about its magnificent headlands and the long crescent of sand beach on the main island. You'll probably find several yachts anchored in Roque Island Harbor or tucked into the small cove on its western edge. Most of the islands in the archipelago are owned by the Gardner family, which has established a research station and private nature conservation area on its holdings. There is no public access in this area, and while yachters may enjoy the beach and protected anchorage, kayakers have been warned off. There is concern that the impact of small-boaters will disturb ongoing research. As always, take care to avoid disturbing nesting sites and seal haul-out areas. Do not land in this area. You could not ask for a more beautiful spot to explore such an easy paddle from a mainland shore, but you'll need to stay in your boat at all times and be sensitive to any wildlife in the area. From your cockpit you can often observe ospreys, bald eagles, seals, and a variety of seabirds that are part of this coastal ecosystem.

You can easily spend a full day exploring throughout this area. It is a short paddle—less than 1.5 miles—from the state beach at Roque Bluffs to the northeastern side of Roque Island. As you paddle along the eastern shores of Marsh and Bar Islands, there are beautiful views to the outer islands of Double Shot, Anguilla, and Halifax (which is managed by U.S. Fish and Wildlife). You can often hear the

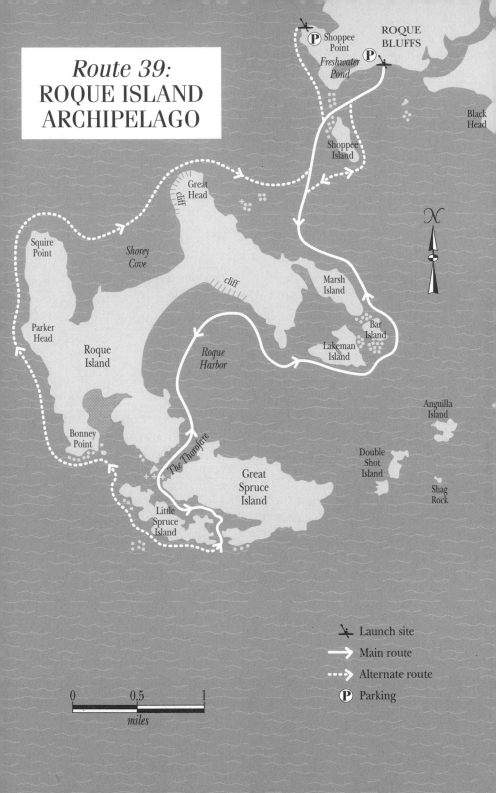

Route 39:
ROQUE ISLAND ARCHIPELAGO

ROQUE BLUFFS

P Shoppee
Point
*Freshwater
Pond*

Black
Head

Shoppee
Island

Great
Head
cliff

*Shorey
Cove*

Squire
Point

cliff

Marsh
Island

Bar
Island

Parker
Head

Roque
Island

*Roque
Harbor*

Lakeman
Island

Anguilla
Island

Bonney
Point

The Thorofare

Double
Shot
Island

Great
Spruce
Island

Shag
Rock

Little
Spruce
Island

N

✕ Launch site
⟶ Main route
⇢ Alternate route
P Parking

0   0.5   1
miles

waves pounding on these islands, even from this distance. This is probably one of the most exhilarating views we have ever had from a sea kayak. The water is remarkably clear, and the incredible textures and colors of ledges beneath your hull make it as fascinating to look down at the water as around at the scenery.

Roque Harbor is a large, protected piece of water with cliffs along the northeast side and an amazing crescent of sandy beach. Paddle out the Thorofare to the western side of Great Spruce Island, and make sure to explore the area between Great Spruce and Little Spruce; it is quiet and protected and offers a relaxing float. Depending on your skills and stamina, you might consider going outside Great Spruce to explore the outer islands, or taking the western route home outside Little Spruce and along the western shore of Roque. Either of these routes may prove demanding, so be prepared to simply backtrack through the harbor to home. There can be some serious wave energy spent along these outer shores, and the rebound from this can create very confusing conditions. Do not undertake this without good bracing skills and an understanding of wave dynamics. Shorey Cove, on the northwest side of Roque, is the island's boat anchorage; it has several buildings and a large pier. The soaring cliffs at Great Head along the east side of the cove are quite spectacular, and the paddling through here is usually calm.

Keep an eye out for any approaching fog banks. Fog can move in quickly and completely shut down visibility in this area, especially in July and August. This is not a ground fog that burns off with the morning sun; instead, it's the thick advection fog created when the cold waters from the Bay of Fundy meet warm, moist air coming from the southwest. It's a common summer recipe and should always figure in your plans.

A foggy-day alternative is to paddle on Gardner Lake just outside Machias. To reach this, turn left onto the paved road 5.3 miles north of Helen's Restaurant, then turn right to reach the large parking area 0.5 mile beyond.

TRIP HIGHLIGHTS: Magnificent headlands, bald eagles, ospreys, seals, and unbelievable views to the outer islands.

TRIP DURATION/LENGTH: A circle of Roque Island, through the Thorofare and around Little Spruce Island, is almost 12 miles long. However, you'll probably enjoy paddling within the harbor and exploring the smaller islands and exposed ledges that dot both eastern and western edges of this archipelago, so mileage can range from 8 to 20 miles, depending on your curiosity and stamina. If you choose to backtrack instead of continuing along the western and northern shores of Roque Island, you'll cut a mile or more off your trip depending on whether you circumnavigate Little Spruce Island or not. If seas are running up Chandler Bay or there is a strong westerly blowing or foggy conditions, this would be the better route home. Remember that there are no places to land on the islands of this archipelago. Be prepared to stay in your boat for the long haul or make a return trip to the mainland for a break.

NAVIGATIONAL AIDS: Chart 13326 Machias Bay to Tibbett Narrows (1:40,000). Boundary Ledges buoy; Roque Island Ledge buoy.

CAUTIONS: Fog and more fog. Exposed conditions along the western shore of Roque Island and anywhere outside of Double Shot, Anguilla, and Halifax Islands.

LAUNCH SITE: Roque Bluffs State Park is located on the mainland shore and offers an easy launch from its beach. This state park encompasses 274 acres with several hiking trails that range from 0.3 to 2.1 miles in length. There is ample parking as well as rest room facilities, grills, and picnic tables. A $1.00-per-person fee is charged. This is a unique spot, with a saltwater beach on one side and a freshwater pond just a few steps away for a choice in swimming. With the two habitats side by side, bird-watching here is unusually good. Use Roque Bluffs as a base for day trips in this area and a convenient rest stop as you come and go during your kayaking explorations.

To reach the park, take Route 1 from Jonesport toward Machias, and look for a large, brown ROQUE BLUFFS STATE PARK sign shortly after you cross the Chandler River. Follow this road down to a stop sign, turn right onto Roque Bluffs Road, and continue down to the well-maintained picnic and swimming area on your right. It is an easy carry across the road and down to the beach. There is no overnight parking or camping.

There is also a town boat ramp where Roque Bluffs Road ends at the waters of Great Cove. This is a steep launch ramp that can be used at all tides. Limited parking is available on the right-hand side of the road. Please do not park along the building on the left side of the road; this is private property.

LOCAL ATTRACTIONS: To the south, Jonesport offers a couple of small lodging establishments: Tootsie's Bed and Breakfast (207–497–5414) and Harbor House on Sawyer Cove (207–497–5417). To the north, Machias offers several motels like the Machias Motor Inn (207–255–4861) and there's Helen's Restaurant. Roque Bluffs State Park has hiking trails that range from 0.3 to 2.1 miles in length. There are also picnic facilities and a freshwater pond for swimming.

Route 40

Englishman River

This short, limited jaunt from the Roque Bluffs beach can only be undertaken on the upper half of the tide, but it's a very nice paddle nonetheless. It offers great wind protection and is rich in birds, which feed among the mudflats and gravel bars along its course. There's little current to contend with and the going is always shallow; don't push your luck with the tide, or you'll have a nasty return leg to open water. This easy route makes a nice "Sunday drive" when combined with a picnic and swim at the state park. In late May and early June, this stretch of water can be very buggy on a day with no breeze.

You can also paddle beyond the Englishman River and round the headlands into Little Kennebec Bay. Try this only if there is little swell running from the south and the wind is not offshore or particularly strong from any direction. There is a short but exposed stretch of paddling that can turn rough quickly because of the long fetch. You'll find a couple of small coves to pop into for some protection, but a strong southwesterly breeze will make it tough to exit and continue on your course.

TRIP HIGHLIGHTS: A quiet stretch of water full of bird life that's a great family trip or foggy day alternative.

TRIP DURATION/LENGTH: We've never been able to get more than a couple of miles upriver—though we haven't yet tried exploring the Englishman on a spring high tide. If you launch from the town ramp into Great Cove you'll add a mile or more each way, depending on whether there's enough water to allow crossing the bar to Shoppee Island.

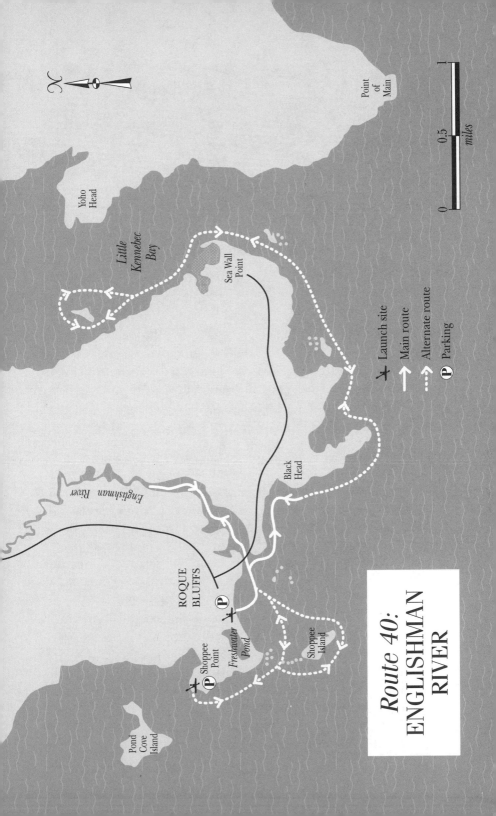

Route 40: ENGLISHMAN RIVER

Point of Main

Yoho Head

Little Kennebec Bay

Sea Wall Point

Englishman River

ROQUE BLUFFS

Black Head

Shoppee Point

Freshwater Pond

Shoppee Island

Pond Cove Island

Launch site
Main route
Alternate route
Parking

1
0.5
0
miles

NAVIGATIONAL AIDS: Chart 13326 Machias Bay to Tibbett Narrows (1:40,000).

CAUTIONS: Mudflats and being stranded on an ebbing tide.

LAUNCH SITE: You can launch from Roque Bluffs and paddle under the small bridge into the Englishman River adjacent to the eastern end of the beach. To reach Roque Bluffs from Jonesport, take Route 1 north toward Machias until you see the large brown ROQUE BLUFFS STATE PARK sign shortly after you cross the Chandler River. Follow this road down to a stop sign, turn right onto Roque Bluffs Road, and continue down to the well-maintained picnic and swimming area on your right. It is an easy carry across the road and down to the beach. No overnight parking or camping is allowed.

There is also a town boat ramp where Roque Bluffs Road ends at the waters of Great Cove. Limited parking is available on the right-hand side of the road. Please do not park along the building on the left side of the road; this is private property. This is a steep launch ramp that can be used at all tides. If you use this launch site you'll need to paddle around Shoppee Point and along Roque Bluffs to reach the mouth of the Englishman River.

LOCAL ATTRACTIONS: To the south, Jonesport offers a couple of small lodging establishments: Tootsie's Bed and Breakfast (207–497–5414) and Harbor House on Sawyer Cove (207–497–5417). To the north, Machias offers several motels like the Machias Motor Inn (207–255–4861) and there's Helen's Restaurant. Roque Bluffs State Park has hiking trails that range from 0.3 to 2.1 miles in length. There are also picnic facilities and a freshwater pond for swimming.

Englishman River

Appendix A

Recommended Reading

Sea Kayaking Instruction

The Complete Book of Sea Kayaking by Derek Hutchinson. The Globe Pequot Press, 1995.

Complete Sea Kayak Touring by Jonathon Hanson. Ragged Mountain Press, 1998.

The Essential Sea Kayaker: A Complete Course for the Open Water Paddler by David Seidman. Ragged Mountain Press, 1992.

Guide to Expedition Kayaking on Seas and Open Water by Derek Hutchinson. The Globe Pequot Press, 1995.

Sea Kayaking by Nigel Foster. The Globe Pequot Press, 1990.

Sea Kayaking: A Manual for Long Distance Touring by John Dowd. University of Washington Press, 1997.

Sea Kayaking: A Woman's Guide by Shelley Johnson. Ragged Mountain Press, 1998.

Seamanship and Weather

Chapman Piloting: Seamanship and Small Boat Handling, by Elbert S. Muloney. William Morrow & Co., 1996.

Fundamentals of Kayak Navigation by David Burch. The Globe Pequot Press, 1993.

Navigational Rules: International and Inland. Gordon Press, 1997.

Sea Kayaker's Deep Trouble: True Stories and Their Lessons from Sea Kayaker Magazine by Matt Broze and Chris Cunningham. Ragged Mountain Press, 1997.

Waves and Beaches by Willard Bascom. Doubleday Press, 1980.

Weather for the Mariner by William J. Kotsch. Naval Institute Press, 1983.

Low-Impact Technique

Backwoods Ethics: Environmental Issues for Hikers and Campers by Laura and Guy Waterman. Countryman Press, 1993.

How to Shit in the Woods by Kathleen Meyer. Ten Speed Press, 1994.

Leave No Trace: Outdoor Skills and Ethics—Temperate Coastal Zones. National Outdoor Leadership School, 1993.

Maine Island Trail Association (MITA) Guidebook published by MITA, annual membership benefit.

Soft Paths: How to Enjoy Wilderness Without Harming It by Bruce Hampton and David Cole. Stackpole Books, 1988.

Natural History

A Birder's Guide to Maine by Elizabeth Pierson, Jan Erik Pierson, and Peter Vickery. Downeast Books, 1996.

Coastal Maine: A Maritime History by Roger F. Duncan. W. W. Norton & Co., 1992.

The Edge of the Sea by Rachel Carson. Houghton Mifflin, 1998.

A Field Guide to Birds of Eastern and Central North America by Roger Tory Peterson. Houghton Mifflin, 1980.

A Field Guide to the Whales, Porpoises, and Seals of the Gulf of Maine and Eastern Canada by Steven K. Katona, Valerie Rough, and David T. Richardson. Charles Scribner's Sons, 1983.

Glaciers and Granite by David L. Kendall. Downeast Books, 1987.

Life on Intertidal Rocks: A Guide to Marine Life on the Rocky North Atlantic Coast. Nature Study Guild, 1987.

Islands in Time: A Human and Natural History of the Islands of Maine by Philip Conkling. Downeast Books, 1998.

Maine Forever: A Guide to Nature Conservancy Preserves in Maine by Ruth Ann Hill. The Nature Conservancy, 1989.

The National Audubon Society Field Guide to New England by Peter Alden et al. Chanticleer Press, 1998.

Roadside Geology of Maine by D. W. Caldwell. Mountain Press, 1998.

Trees and Shrubs of New England by Marilyn Dwelley. Downeast Books, 1980.

Guidebooks

Cruising Guide to Maine (2 vols.) by Don Johnson. Wescott Cove
    Publishing, 1995.

A Cruising Guide to the Maine Coast by Hank Taft, Jan Taft, and Curtis
    Rindlaub. Diamond Pass Publishing, 1996.

Hot Showers! Maine Coast Lodgings for Kayakers and Sailors by Lee Bumsted.
    Audenreed Press, 2000.

Kayaking the Maine Coast by Dorcas Miller. Backcountry Guides, 2000.

The Sea Kayaker's Guide to Mount Desert Island by Jennifer Alisa Paigen.
    Downeast Books, 1997.

Sea Kayaking Along the New England Coast by Tamsin Venn. Appalachian
    Mountain Club, 1991.

Appendix B

Sea Kayaking Outfitters *and* Guide Services *in* Maine

The following businesses offer sea kayaking guide service and instruction in Maine. Some also offer rentals of sea kayaks (to qualified paddlers), NOAA charts, sea kayaking gear, and shuttle services. The list begins in Casco Bay and continues east. Many of these businesses are members of the Maine Association of Sea Kayak Guides and Instructors (MASKGI). For more information on MASKGI members, visit www.maineseakayakguides.com.

Maine Island Kayak Company
70 Luther Street
Peak's Island, ME 04108
1–800–796–2373
207–766–2373
www.maineislandkayak.com

L. L. Bean Outdoor
Discovery Program
Casco Street
Freeport, ME 04032
1–888–552–3261
www.llbean.com/odp

H₂Outfitters
P.O. Box 72
Orrs Island, ME 04066
1–800–20–KAYAK
207–833–5257
www.H2Outfitters.com

Seaspray Kayaking
New Meadows Marina
Brunswick, ME 04011
1–888–349–SPRAY
207–443–3646

Dragonworks, Inc.
42 Stevens Road
Bowdoinham, ME 04008
207–882–7323

Frozen Paddler
Box 271 Old Bath Road
Wiscasset, ME 04578
207–882–9066

Tidal Transit
P.O. Box 743
Boothbay Harbor, ME 04538
207–633–7140

Poseidon Kayak Imports
60 Poseidon Lane
Walpole, ME 04573
207–644–8329
www.nvo.com/poseidonkayaks

Wild Bill's Outfitting and Guide
Service
Outsider's Inn
4 Main Street
Friendship, ME 04547
207–832–5197

Maine Sport Outfitters
Route 1
P.O. Box 956
Rockport, ME 04856
1–800–722–0826
207–236–8797
www.mainesport.com

Camden Kayak
20 Conway Road
Camden, ME 04843
207–236–7709
www.stormloader.com/
camdenkayak

Kennebec Kayak
R.R. 3, Box 990
Winthrop, ME 04364
207–377–2788

Ducktrap Sea Kayak
R.R. 3, Box 3315
Lincolnville, ME 04849
207–236–8608

Sea Kayaking with New England
Outdoor Center
Dennett's Wharf
Castine, ME 04421
1–800–766–7238
www.neoc.com

Granite Island Guide Service
R.R. 1, Box 610A
Deer Isle, ME 04627
207–348–2668
www.maineguides.com/members/
granite

Old Quarry Charters
R.R. 1, Box 700
Stonington, ME 04681
207–266–7778
www.oldquarrycharters.com

The Phoenix Centre
Route 175
Blue Hill Falls, ME 04615
207–374–2113

Maine Coast Experience
H.C. 64, Box 380
Brooklin, ME 04616
1–888–559–5057
207–359–5057
www.mainecoastexperience.com

Coastal Kayaking Tours
48 Cottage Street
P.O. Box 405
Bar Harbor, ME 04609
1–800–526–8615
207–288–9605
www.acadiafun.com

Island Adventures Sea Kayaking
137 Cottage Street
Bar Harbor, ME 04609
207–288–3886

National Park Sea Kayak Tours
29 Cottage Street
P.O. Box 6105
Bar Harbor, ME 04609
1–800–347–0940
207–288–0342
www.acadiakayak.com

Yakman Adventures
P.O. Box 946
Southwest Harbor, ME 04679
Town Dock House
Rice Road
Bernard, ME 04612
207–244–3333
www.yakmanadventures.com

Loon Bay Kayak Tours
P.O. Box 391
Orland, ME 04472
1–888–786–0676
207–266–8888

Moose Look Guide Service
H.C. 35, Box 246
Gouldsboro, ME 04607
207–963–7720

Schoodic Tours
General Delivery
Corea, ME 04624
207–963–7958

Eastern Outdoor Adventures
Route 1
Machias, ME 04654
207–255–4210

Machias Bay Boat Tours and Sea
Kayaking
P.O. Box 42
Machias, ME 04654
207–259–3338
www.machiasbay.com

Sunrise County Canoe and Kayak
Route 1, Machias
H.C. 68, Box 154
Grove, ME 04657
207–454–7708

Tidal Trails Eco-Tours
P.O. Box 321
Leighton Point Road
Pembroke, ME 04666
207–726–4799
207–853–7373
www.nemaine.com/tidaltrails

Appendix C

Resources

What follows is contact information that might be useful to sea kayakers in Maine. *(All area codes are 207 unless otherwise noted.)*

U.S. Coast Guard:

Portland	799–1680
Boothbay Harbor	633–2643
Rockland	596–6666
Southwest Harbor	244–5121
Jonesport	497–5700
Eastport	853–2845

Note: For emergency calls, the Coast Guard may be contacted by VHF radio Channel 16 or by cellular phone at *CG.

Maine State Police:

Southern Maine	1–800–482–0730
Brunswick to Belfast	1–800–452–4664
Belfast to Eastport	1–800–432–7381

Note: For emergency calls, the Maine State Police may be reached by cellular phone at *77.

Other emergency numbers:

Local Emergency Services	911
Poison Control Center	1–800–442–6305
Fire	1–888–900–FIRE (3473)
Red Tide Hotline	1–800–232–4733

Marine Mammal Strandings:

Kittery to Rockland:	Northeast Marine Lifeline	851–6625
	New England Aquarium	617–973–5200
Rockland to Eastport:	College of the Atlantic	288–5644

Harbormasters:

Portland:	772–8121
Falmouth:	781–7317
Yarmouth:	846–3333
Freeport:	865–4546
Brunswick:	725–6631
Bath:	443–5563
Phippsburg:	389–1304
Wiscasset:	882–7230
Boothbay:	633–5281
Rockland:	594–0312
Camden:	236–7969
Lincolnville:	763–3983
Belfast:	338–1142
Bucksport:	469–7952
Stonington:	367–5585
Bar Harbor:	288–5571
Southwest Harbor:	244–7913
Northeast Harbor:	276–5111
Tremont (Seal Cove):	244–5464
Milbridge:	546–7251
Jonesport:	497–5931

Commercial Organizations

Maine Campground Association:	782–5874
	www.campmaine.com
Maine Innkeeper's Association:	773–7670
	www.maineinns.com

Governmental and Non-Profit Organizations

Maine Island Trail Association:	761–8225 (Portland)
	596–6456 (Rockland)
	www.mita.org
Acadia National Park:	288–5463
	www.nps.gov/acad/

Maine State Office of Tourism:	www.visitmaine.com
Maine Audubon Society:	781–2330
	www.maineaudubon.org
Maine Coast Heritage Trust	729–7366
	www.mcht.org
Maine Land Trust Network:	729–7366
	www.mltn.org
The Nature Conservancy	729–5181
	www.tnc.org/maine
Appalachian Mountain Club:	617–523–0636
	www.outdoors.org
Leave No Trace:	www.lnt.org

Paddling Clubs

Penobscot Paddle and Chowder Society
1115 North Main Street
Brewer, ME 04412

Southern Maine Sea Kayaking Network
P.O. Box 4794
Portland, ME 04112-4794
874–2640
www.smskn.org
outdoors@gwi.net

About the Authors

Shelley Johnson and Vaughan Smith have been exploring and kayaking Maine's waterways for the past fifteen years. They are both Registered Maine Guides and American Canoe Association (ACA) certified coastal kayaking instructors. They co-produced the sea kayak safety video *What Now? Sea Kayak Rescue Techniques*, and are partners in a paddlesports marketing company, Powerface, Inc., based in Maine.

Shelley has written for *Atlantic Coastal Kayaker*, *Adventure Journal*, and *Kayak Touring*, and was for a number of years sea kayak editor for *Canoe and Kayak* magazine. She is also the author of *Sea Kayaking: A Woman's Guide*.

As avid paddlers committed to water trail development and island conservation, Shelley and Vaughan are eager to share with others those special places and seascapes that can only be enjoyed from the unique perspective of a sea kayak.